ROOTS OF TIME

The aim of Zenith Books is to present the history of minority groups in the United States and their participation in the growth and development of the country. Through histories and biographies written by leading historians in collaboration with established writers for young people, Zenith Books will increase awareness of and at the same time develop an understanding and appreciation for minority group heritage.

DR. JOHN HOPE FRANKLIN, Chairman of the History Department at the University of Chicago, has also taught at Brooklyn College, Fisk University, and Howard University. For the year 1962–63, he was William Pitt Professor of American History and Institutions at Cambridge University in England. He is the author of many books, including *From Slavery to Freedom, The Militant South, Reconstruction After the Civil War,* and *The Emancipation Proclamation.*

MARGO JEFFERSON is an Associate Editor at *Newsweek* magazine. She has written articles for the Washington *Post, Harper's Magazine* and *MS.* magazine. She is currently working on a children's book.

DR. ELLIOTT P. SKINNER is presently Chairman of the Anthropology Department at Columbia University. He has traveled throughout Africa, South America, and Europe, and has done field work in British Guiana (Guyana), French West Africa, and Upper Volta. He served as United States Ambassador to Upper Volta from 1966 to 1969. Dr. Skinner has authored numerous books and articles on African peoples and cultures.

JERRY PINCKNEY was born in Philadelphia, Pennsylvania. He attended the Philadelphia Museum College of Art. Mr. Pinckney has illustrated many children's books—among them *Kasho & the Twin Flutes* and *Femi and Old Grandaddie,* two African children's tales. He is the recipient of the 1973 award from the Society of Illustrators.

ROOTS OF TIME

309.16
J

A Portrait of African Life and Culture

7/71

By MARGO JEFFERSON
and ELLIOTT P. SKINNER

Illustrated by Jerry Pinckney

ZENITH BOOKS
Doubleday & Company, Inc., Garden City, New York   1974

The Zenith Books edition, published simultaneously in hardbound and paper-
back volumes, is the first publication of *Roots of Time*.

Zenith Books Edition: 1974

Library of Congress Cataloging in Publication Data
Jefferson, Margo.
Roots of time: portrait of African life and culture.
SUMMARY: Discusses various aspects of birth,
childhood, economics, marriage, family relationships,
politics, society, religion, and art common to many
native African people.
1. Ethnology—Africa—Juvenile literature.
2. Africa—Civilization—Juvenile literature.
3. Africa—History—Juvenile literature. [1. Ethnology—
Africa. 2. Africa—Civilization] I. Skinner, Elliott
Percival, 1924–   joint author. II. Pinckney, Jerry,
illus. III. Title.
GN645.J43 1974   916'.03
ISBN 0-385-07731-0 TRADE
0-385-07731-9 PAPERBOUND
LIBRARY OF CONGRESS CATALOG CARD NUMBER 74–1511

CONTENTS

African Societies

1. Dogon	9. Yoruba	17. Batwa
2. Mende	10. Igbo	18. Rwanda
3. Mossi	11. Kalabari	19. Swahili
4. Fulani	12. Zande	20. Tonga
5. Hausa	13. Sidamo	21. Luvale
6. Tiv	14. Jie	22. Kung Bushmen
7. Ashanti	15. Masai	23. Lovedu
8. Fanti	16. Gikuyu	24. Zulu

1

INTRODUCTION

Africa. The word brings to mind a thousand pictures—of deep green forests, mighty rivers, dry bare deserts, and wide expanses of rich farmland; or majestic animals moving across the plains unhindered by cages with bars; of snow-capped mountains and deep valleys; of small villages with huts and towns with marketplaces; of large bustling cities with tall buildings and constant activity. Much has been said and written about this huge (nearly twelve million square miles) and ancient continent—some false, some true. Africa, sun-covered and wonderfully tropical, spans the horizons of light and has sheltered the rise and fall of mighty civilizations, from the Pharaohs of Egypt to the Ashanti of Ghana. Many believe it to be the "cradle of civilization," the birthplace of the first humans.

Africa may have been mysterious often just because it contains so much life—plant, animal, and human. Africa has rainy tropics, but it also has the world's largest desert. It has the world's largest lake as well, and the powerful Nile and Congo rivers. Almost anything that can be said of Africa has its opposite, which is also true. The continent receives more sun than almost any other in the world, and yet parts of it are constantly drenched with rain. Dynasties and kingdoms have arisen there; but Africa has small wandering groups of people, nomads leading the simplest of lives.

Life in Africa is, traditionally, bound to the land which, like a friend, must be cooperated with, treated well, and outwitted from time to time. The hardy !Kung live in the Kalahari Desert areas of Botswana, and so they hunt and gather. The small Batwa live in the Zaire forests and are expert hunters, setting up "camps" of huts that last as long as the hunting is good, and then moving on to other parts of the forest. When they need food or other supplies that the forest does not offer, they go to nearby agricultural villages and exchange products on a practical, if not always friendly, basis. Some people, such as the Bozo of Mali and the Ebrie of the Ivory Coast, fish along the rivers, lakes, and lagoons; others grow food on the savanna and forest lands. Some people keep cattle on the rolling velds. The Fulani of Nigeria and Masai of Kenya and Tanzania live comfortably in these areas. Where grass or *forage* is scarce, groups like the North African Bedouins and the Somali keep camels, which are famed for their ability to live on the smallest amounts of food and water. The Tiv, Igbo, and Hausa of Nigeria and the Swazi of Swaziland are farmers—a livelihood for many Africans—and they tend their crops on the fairly dry savanna land and in the wet rainforests. There are crops of millet, plantains, bananas, maize, cocoa, peanuts, cassava, and many others. One might think that so many people, making a living in so many different ways, would become suspicious of each other and fearful that someone "over there" was taking away their land and their cattle or crops. But Africans know that survival is much harder where bickering occurs, and they also know that the continent is huge and the land around is plentiful, so why shouldn't fishers, herders, and hunters all live and work in the area? Hunters and gatherers and fisherfolk exchange products with herders and farmers. So the Hausa farmer welcomes the presence of the Fulani herder, because those herds fertilize his land.

People, animals, and plants in Africa—how did they live together nearly two million years ago? How did some animals who lived by instinct on plants and other animals slowly become men and women who thought and invented objects and methods that gave them more "control" over nature? Stones were probably the link. The apes that roamed the eastern part of the continent evolved to man-apes (Australopithecines) when they began using the stones around them to make tools. Pebble tools were found scattered over the "living floor" of the homes of *homo habilis*, an early form of man. These tools were probably used for defense against other animals. Later they were used for killing animals as food as the savanna home of early man with its dry grass, shallow lakes, and long, dry seasons failed to produce enough supplies of vegetables for him to live on. Stone tools developed over the centuries in Africa gave these wandering hunters and gatherers a new way of surviving in their tropical world, a way that could be passed on to their descendants, and developed, and changed, giving birth at last to whole new ways of life and whole new civilizations.

Early men and women moved across the savannas in southern, eastern, and northern Africa, and after a time moved into the rich central forests. Some hunted; some fished; some farmed. When one group met another they fought, or mingled and joined together. And so more groups of people emerged, and new ways of living came about. Some people wandered constantly; others settled and built their lives in one place. Whether traveling or settling, these groups changed steadily, always exploring and experimenting with ways of adapting to new ecological demands. African peoples moved across the continent on foot, following trails and water courses, even through the Sahara Desert, which was not always as dry or barren as it is today.

More and greater differences grew up between groups of men and women as they spread across the land. The first few languages grew into many—eight hundred or more —and yet the common roots remain. All eight hundred languages can be placed into four large major families, which though related, also show their differences. The *Afro-Asian* family suggests the links between the early Africans and Asians many years ago. Hausa, ancient Egyptian, Hebrew, and Arabic are four languages of this family spoken in and on the borders of Africa. Then there are the Congo-Kordofanian languages. These dominate the continent, from West to Central, East, and South Africa, and they include the many Bantu languages. The small family of Nilo-Saharan languages tells a tale of the migrations of many people across vast stretches of Africa. Finally, there are the famous Click languages, with their clicking sounds. These were once widespread, but they are now heard only in South Africa, where they have enriched many Bantu languages.

African populations sometimes mingle and "exchange" languages. The Fulani of West Africa traveled eastward across the Sudan, spreading a language they had acquired in the West, and absorbing both the language and the physical traits of the people among whom they traveled. And the Batwa of the central forest mingle with the agricultural groups in villages around them and have adopted their languages as well. Some Bantu-speaking people of East Africa who met the visiting Arabs developed the Swahili language. This rich, Arabized Bantu language is so widespread in East Africa that it is called a *lingua franca*—a language used in common by many people.

But finding links between the many people of Africa is like playing detective, and following a set of clues through many situations. The surface appearance may be different each time, but the clue itself is the same. For example, Africans outside of the larger towns live in huts. Whether they are round huts made of leaves and branches, easily built, easily left behind, or stick-frame compounds made to house crops and animals, the huts serve the same purpose. They are meant to give shelter, not to be lived in constantly. People all over Africa venerate their ancestors. They believe that they are the link between God and humans. The powerful Queen Mother appears in West Africa as well as in Central and South Africa. Her roots lie in the dynasties of Egypt, when the Pharaoh and his Queen ruled the land. The use of the bride token—gifts brought

13

Many people outside the larger towns live in small villages in huts. These huts are simply designed to give shelter.

to the bride's family by the groom's—is found in all parts of Africa, and the many African social and political organizations seem to be quite similar.

Africa changes and yet remains constant. Like a river fed by many streams, it has a basic flow, yet many smaller, independent branches. It has one long history made up of many shorter histories; many different ways of living but they are all variations of continent-wide African ones. Perhaps change and growth are the realities of African history, because they seem never to stop. The recent European conquests should not blind us to the dynamism of Africa and its peoples. Ancient Africans ventured into or were taken to southern Europe, the Middle East, India, and perhaps farther east. There are some scholars who believe that Africans arrived in the New World even before Columbus. Modern European conquests scattered Africans throughout the New World. Until the nineteenth century there were more Africans than Europeans in North America, Latin America, and the West Indies. The children of Africa were involved in nearly every aspect of life in the expanding New World. They went on exploration expeditions; they fought in battles; as captives, their labor created cotton and sugar cane empires; they worked in factories; they participated in science, politics, education, and art. Their influence is felt in every country in which they settled, and today, many traits of the ancient civilizations from which Africans came are found in the New World. This book will explore them and help you recognize and identify them.

2

BIRTH AND CHILDHOOD

The Abaluyia of Kenya believe that God created everything in the universe, and then wanted a creature for the
sun to shine upon. And so God made the first woman and
the first man. Men and women are the center of the universe, its seed, whose nourishment and growth are linked
to the seasons.

"How was I born?" a child may ask, and the answer
may be, "Your mother fetched you from a pool in the
river." African children are told many tales about birth, because it is a complex, even magical happening, binding the
past to the present, the dead to the living, and the spiritual
to the natural. Children are a blend of their parents and
God. The Ashanti of Ghana believe that a child receives
blood from the mother, character and personality from the
father, and a soul from God. The Kgatala of Botswana
believe that the mother gives blood to the child and the
father gives flesh, and so the child should look more like
the father. No child, though, is merely a son or a daughter
of the earth. All are offspring of God, the Supreme Being,
and all become a part of a family, including parents, sisters,
brothers, cousins, and ancestors, who will surround them

until their death and birth into another life. The birth of a child is the birth of a soul and the continuation of a family.

Childbirth practices vary, but many African mothers, assisted by other women, give birth while bending over or sitting upon a stool, holding a mortar and pestle. Before the child's umbilical cord is cut, he or she is made to touch the ground with hands and feet, taking control of the soul. The child is then cleaned, and for the first time the father visits and places a sign on the door of the home to announce the birth. Now the child is ready to be named, and is taken to the father's relatives and placed on the altar of the ancestors. "Pray God to bring you riches," an elder recites, "pray God to take care of you. The name of this child will be ——, and a name is given. Several days later the child is taken to the mother's family and given a second name. Finally, the priest of the father's family gives the child a third, secret name, one that only the priest may use.

A child cannot be named by chance or by whim. The name must reflect the child's place in the universe and in the family. A child may be named Amene, "Man of God," or "First Born." Children are sometimes named for their ancestors. The Ashanti give a child one name from the mother's family, one from the father's, and one from the day of the week on which the birth took place. A southern African parent may give a child a name that commemorates an event dear and important to him or her. A name may tell whether a child is born first or last, and whether he or she was born soon after marriage or long after the marriage when a couple had given up hope of having a

child. Then such a name given a child is a mark of tri-
umph. Thus a proud mother may call her son "Barama,"
meaning, "There is nothing God cannot do," or "Geta-
mani-go," meaning, "See what I have done!"

The name can be powerful enough to help trick the
spirits intent to do a child harm. It is believed that certain spirits, tricksters, may be born as children to Mossi
mothers in Upper Volta. These tricksters do not intend to
live. They intend to die to hurt the happy mother. What
child is a trickster and what child is not? To protect herself and her child, then, a Mossi mother may give her
child a deliberately bad name, like "Dirty Thing." It is the
first warning to the trickster, who must be beaten at his
own game. The mother plays the game carefully. She takes
"Dirty Thing" to the marketplace, where she is met by a
helpful relative who pretends to "buy" the child away. It
is a ploy to fool the trickster. What mother would willingly
sell her child? The trickster is thwarted; he no longer has
a mother to hurt. So the life of the child is saved from the
malicious intentions of the trickster.

Even without tricksters, childbirth is perilous, and children often die. In many African societies, it is believed
that men and women live many lives and are born many
times. Ancestors return to earth, and the soul lives over and
over. When a child is born, his spirit may change its mind
quickly and decide to return to the other world. Mothers
and fathers wait and hope until a child starts to walk and
talk. Only then can one be sure that the spirit has defi-
nitely decided to remain on Earth.

Mothers rarely give birth casually or untended. Whether

Children are an important part of the African society. A woman who is going to have a child is not left unattended. She is aided by the women of the community.

the mother is with her parents or in her husband's compound, she is surrounded by the women of the community who help and encourage her through labor and birth. A child can carry early memories of being fondled and loved by many women, not only by mother. Mothers feed and watch over their children carefully, nursing them for two to four years, and often not bearing another child until the first is weaned. It is believed that each child should have milk and should not compete for it. A child weaned too soon and forced to "move over" through the birth of another could sicken and even die. Weaning therefore is done naturally, and with nature's help. The mother nurses until her milk dries up, or when she feels the child's time has come she may rub her breasts with bitter leaves, and then offer the child soft, sweet foods like bananas and yams as substitutes. Other children play their part too: more than one boy or girl has been teased into weaning by playmates.

Growing is as natural to children as it is to plants, animals, and other things in nature. Children in Africa are not forced to grow. They are allowed to grow at their own pace in their own rhythm. Toilet training is usually gradual, with children learning from their older sisters or cousins, and their nurses. Their nurses are quick to hold them away from their hips at the proper time. Later on they are taken outside to a secluded spot (perhaps a clump of bushes). Be modest in such matters, they are taught as they grow older. Be discreet; it is thoughtful of those around you, and it is safe. A wicked person may use the feces to bewitch an unsuspecting and careless child.

African childhood, one poet writes, is a time of "dreaming and becoming." Children grow up together. They eat and play together. They are taught by their parents, and they teach one another. Young girls are trained by their older sisters and their mothers; young boys, when they are five or six years old, leave their mothers' house for the boys' compound, where they learn from their fathers and carry messages for the men. Life is enriched by singing and dancing, playing games such as *warri* (a kind of checkers), and with clay animals and string figures. Cooking and hunting games prepare children for later life; the children are lovingly taught to address elders ceremoniously and to receive gifts graciously. A frightening tale, told with excitement, may serve as punishment for a bad child—perhaps a tale of certain children carried away by ruthless monsters. Childhood is where balance is learned, where pleasures and duties exist in equal importance and are often combined. Children learn that they must grow to adulthood, and yet they know that they can enjoy their childhood.

> They haunt me still in work and play;
> those whispering leaves behind the slit
> on the cabin wall of childhood's
> dreaming and becoming.
>
> Byormbeeyi Adali-Mortti

Eventually, every child takes steps into adulthood—important steps, filled with ceremony and meaning. One abandons childhood with rituals of puberty; among some groups these rituals include circumcision for the boys and clitoridectomy for the girls. Among the Masai of Kenya, the Lovedu of South Africa, the Susu of Guinea, or the Bushongo of Zaire, the transition from childhood to adulthood is a time of anxiety and fear. An initiation song of Central Africa learned by boys and girls from their parents tells of this fear.

> Your words produce great fear within us,
> But we cannot run off.
> Yet you, you once were also an initiate
> And obviously you are not the least bit dead:
> So we too shall not die.

The souls of men and women, it is believed by the Dogon at Mali, share certain qualities—qualities that balance each other and so reflect the balance of the universe. There are male qualities and female qualities. There is a male soul and a female soul. But a newborn child is given both, and so all boys have certain qualities of the female soul and all girls certain qualities of the male. Every child carries a twin soul of the opposite sex. To enter the adult world, taking one's proper place in its social and religious life, every boy and girl must regain the full power of their sex. Circumcision eliminates the femaleness from the male body and soul. Clitoridectomy takes the maleness from the female self. And the child takes on his or her sex in all of its original force, thus becoming a full man or woman.

Ceremonies leading to adulthood are mysterious and awesome, with the adults of each sex teaching the young, and calling on their own ancestors to witness and inspire. Among the males, boys aged ten to fourteen are taken

To become an adult in the eyes of the society each girl and boy must participate in the ceremonies of adulthood.

from the village to a special lodge. The ceremony of the "uninitiated" may begin each night after a feast and after the sun has set. It is a long, challenging preparation, lasting six weeks perhaps. The young boys learn the legends and history of their people; they are taught singing and dancing. In Mali, Dogon boys stay at the lodge all of the time. In Upper Volta, Mossi girls return to the village at night, leaving each morning. There are many rituals; daytime rituals and nighttime rituals. There is the "Ceremony of the Lions," chants, lessons, feasts. And the children are not told the full meaning of what they learn until the day of their initiation, the day when they become adults and members of the society. Why are they kept in such mystery? Camara Laye of Guinea, in his book *The Dark Child*, writes that without the mystery, the religious and social teaching would not be the same, "nothing would remain of the trial by fear, that occasion when every boy has the opportunity to overcome his fear and his own baser nature." Initiation is a test for the spirit as well as the body.

After circumcision, the new men and women live in the lodge for three months. They speak a special language, they talk of special things. They learn of hunting, they learn of sex. They are taught courage and endurance; sometimes the youth are beaten. When they return to the village, they return as grownups. There, they meet grown men and women who have taken a different but similar journey. Growth is an endless process in African societies traditionally, one that carries people past death and into another life. Puberty is only one step in this progression, as birth was only the first step of life.

In many places children enter "age sets," a group or class formed at puberty, and remain in them all their lives, moving together through the "grades" of adulthood. As the members of these age classes, young boys become young men, middle-aged men, senior men. Young girls become young women, wives and mothers, senior women. At each step, they, naturally, perform different tasks. Liberia's age sets are elaborate. They are first formed in the schools or "bushes"—the Poro for men, the Sande for women. The initiates or members of these sets are so important that they often govern the communities. South Africans too teach their children through initiation schools. To them, growth is not a chance occurrence; it is a series of stages, clearly marked. The spiritual and the natural forces, ancestors and gods, must help men and women to travel through these stages; ceremonies summon their powers, striving to correct the faults and break the restrictions of previous stages. Who does not know the fear of being too young or too childish to meet the challenge that life is about to offer? The South Africans understand that one does not have to fight unreadiness alone. Without spiritual forces, one's life, they say, can be soured. With spiritual forces, good may follow, and the next stage may be reached in due time. Then the duties and privileges of life are taught and learned.

The old and the young are brought together when the time comes to initiate and instruct the young. Men wanting to become warriors are taught by older men, learning bravery, by experience. Women are taught by older women, living with them and studying their ways, receiving sexual training from them. Among the Zulu in South Africa, the boys form regiments upon leaving training school. Both men and women emerge from initiation to form age classes or sets. Once a class, they go through life together. Some sets or classes are named after animals (for example, "Age Class of the Leopard") and some after events (for example, "Age Class of the Storm"). Some age sets or classes reappear regularly. For example, the Age Class of the Leopard may first hunt or herd after leaving school. They do this together for many years, then they all move into another activity. Now they are in the grade of warriors. Years pass, and their warrior days end. They move to the rank of junior elders. Finally, they become senior elders. Those who have survived join the grade of priests. After a long time, perhaps eighty years, the Age Class of the Leopard is reborn, like the individual who goes from birth to death to rebirth. In some societies, like the Galla of Ethiopia, when the time comes for the new set to start, the survivors come out and rejoin as though they were youngsters. But long before the age set moves out of childhood, they die and join their ancestors.

3

ECONOMIC SYSTEMS

African peoples have learned to make their living using the rich variety of plant and animal life in the mountains, rivers, plains, forests, and deserts of their continent. Animals often forced people to use all of their ingenuity to earn a living. Perhaps, because of so many contrasts, so many forms of life, African peoples live in harmony with their environments. They know much about the habits of animals and the values and uses of plants. They have also learned to respect the mysteries of nature and can be "scientific" or mythical about a plant's flowering, an animal's movements, or the rotating of the sun and the moon. One cannot know everything about the universe and its workings, but one respects and honors them, often thinking about living within the order that exists.

For most Africans, land is more than a source of wealth; it is sacred. It gives people life, and so they believe that they were entrusted with it and must, in return, treasure it. The Kikuyu believe that Ngai or God took their first ancestor to the top of Mount Kenya, from which forests of cedars, olives, and bamboo trees could be seen, as well as rivers, plains with antelope and buffalo herds, and the snow-capped peaks of high mountains. Ngai gave all of this to Kikuyu, who promised to act according to his will all his life. Ngai then promised this "good and brave warrior" that "within the great bowl formed by the mountains, your sons and daughters shall roam and multiply. You shall enjoy the beauty of the country and all its fruits. Always remember that it is I who have bestowed this upon you. My blessing shall be with you and your offspring wherever you go."

Likewise, those people in Africa who herd cattle honor the Creator for the land upon which their flocks feed. The Sotho of South Africa sing a song of praise to God in which the Almighty says:

> I, the revered of all nations,
> I, forever the same,
> I, the leader to pastures and guide back to the kraal,
> I, the origin of all sustenance,
> I am the mother of all nurture,
> 'Tis I that reign, father of all bounty,
> I, the bellow of the bull,
> Ye are fed, ye are satisfied.

So men and women consider the land, crops, and animals an ancient gift of God. Each society has myths and legends that describe how it received these gifts differently. But God did not offer gifts to one group alone. The Kikuyu say that God had three sons, and that to the first he gave the arrow, making him the Ndorobo hunter; to the second he gave the cattle, making him the Masai herder; and to the third he gave the hoe, making him the Kikuyu farmer. We do not know if the Ndorobo were granted all animals, but the Kikuyu tried to keep all of their land and get more, while the Masai believe that, symbolically, they are custodians of all the world's cattle.

The Zulu of South Africa believe that Unkulunkulu, the old old one, was the first being on earth. But after he sprang from a reed, all people, plants, and animals came to life with him. Unkulunkulu looked about him, named the sun as a torch to light the way for people, and gave them the cattle to keep and milk, the wild animals to hunt, and the fire to cook by. Finally, he declared, "Let there be marriage among men, that there may be those who can intermarry, that children may be born and men increase on earth."

The early Africans hunted animals and gathered vegetables and fruits to live on. Today, only the !Kung and the Batwa remain hunters and gatherers solely, and in times of drought, they must turn to their farming and herding neighbors for help. To the Batwa in Zaire the forest is both mother and father, giving them food, shelter, and comfort. They hunt using many different kinds of plant poisons and arrows, as well as nets. They move from place to place in the forest, knowing from long experience what paths animals follow and what areas contain the greenest plants and the ripest fruits. And yet, this skill and knowledge are not enough. The Batwa believe that the forest is a moral environment as well as a physical one, and when people are evil, the forest will not provide them with food. One is not fed well if one does not live well, and so a way of life that tries to control evil and atone for it fairly must be found by forest people.

The Masai of Kenya—a herding people—believe symbolically that they are custodians of all the world's cattle.

In Botswana the !Kung do not have the same attitude toward the Kalahari Desert, but they know it well. !Kung hunters must be able to recognize the tracks of one wildebeest wounded in a herd of fifty, and they must follow its tracks across the stone-hard desert ground. To hunt the large ostrich, !Kung hunters disguise themselves as ostriches, moving with almost total silence among the large birds.

Food is distributed equally and fairly among both the !Kung and the Batwa: No one is left out because he or she is useless, unworthy, or too old to hunt. Those who cannot hunt often give arrows to the hunters, and are later given the animals killed with these arrows. Food taboos are set up among hunting groups, necessary both to maintain the number of live animals and to see that all people are fed equally. Batwa hunters watch over the animals they hunt, and will not let men with more than one wife eat certain animals whose population is rather small. Such practical habits become bound up with a group's myths and legends. There are stories which relate that a certain family does not eat a certain animal because, at the world's beginning, that animal saved the first ancestor's life.

Hunting no longer has the central place in most African societies that it once did, but its ritual and dignity remain. To the Luvale of Zambia who farm, the hunter is still the brave man, the gallant man, the man who faces danger. Meat is special in a predominantly vegetable and grain diet, and it is distributed with care and ceremony. Certain parts of the hunt go to the hunter's mother's brother; certain parts go to the chiefs; certain parts go to the people.

When hunting ostrich in the Kalahari Desert, the !Kung hunters move
silently among their prey.

Likewise, though gathering is no longer the main source of food for most African people, it has a continued place in day-to-day life. Meat is a specialty. Fruits, nuts, shrubs, and vegetables are eaten constantly and also used for medicine and in ceremonies. Not to gather these items would be to ignore the environment!

A larger number of African peoples are pastoralists or herders, although they total no more than 10 percent of all the societies. In West Africa the Fulani are the only real herders, keeping their herds in a band of territory from Senegal to the northern Cameroons. Herders are travelers, moving continuously across the grasslands to find water. The Fulani move toward the forest regions during the dry season, and back to the Sudan for the rainy season, fertilizing the fields of their farmer neighbors with their cattle and taking grain and vegetables from them in exchange. Most African herders live in East Africa. Chief among them are the Masai, who herd their cattle, sheep, and goats on the plains of Kenya and Tanzania. There are the Jie of Uganda, and the Dinka and Nuer of the Sudan. The Kababish Arabs herd camels in the Sudan, as well as sheep, goats, and cattle. The women milk the herds and the men tend them.

Like the hunters who see a moral and spiritual life in the forest that yields them food, many herders make the cattle a part of the songs that they sing and the legends, myths, and stories they tell. Among the Nuer, young boys are given cows to tend, and while caring for them, sing of their beauty. These boys know the varieties of cows, the unique features of each (as the young American boys praise and care for their first cars, discussing them with friends and boasting about them to acquaintances). A song of praise to a cow leads to other thoughts: thoughts of kinsmen and thoughts of love.

> White ox good is my mother
> And we the people of my sister,
> The people of Nyariau Bul.
> As my black-rumped white ox,
> When I went to court the winsome lassie,
> I am not a man whom girls refuse.
> We court girls by stealth in the night,
> I and Kwejok
> Nyadeang.
> We brought the ox across the river,
> I and Kirjoak
> And the son of my mother's sister
> Buth Gutjaak.
> Friend, great ox of the spreading horns,
> Which ever bellows amid the herd,
> Ox of the son of Bul
> Maloa.

In some regions of Africa, herders, hunters, and farmers live together and exchange products, depending upon each other for survival. In Ruanda, the Batwa and some Hutu hunt to live while the Tutsi hunt for sport. The Batwa hunt irregularly, because the hunt is not always good: They have to depend, sometimes, upon the generosity of their neighbors, singing and dancing for them, receiving food in return. The Hutu give the Tutsi vegetables, in exchange for milk and meat, but the Tutsi do not like to feel indebted to the Hutu and so drink a good deal of milk from their cows to show their independence and to insist upon their natural and basic difference.

As one would expect, land is important and has spiritual and moral meaning to the many African farming populations. The use of land, called *usufruct*, was closely linked to most of the religious and kinship institutions of these societies. The Kikuyu viewed the earth as the mother, feeding her children throughout their lives and nursing their spirits after death. If a person swears by the earth, that oath is an everlasting one. The earth is more sacred than any creature that dwells in it or on it. The Mossi contrast earth to men and women: One is eternal, the other dies. To them, too, earth is the mother, and the words for land—*Tenga, Tempoko*, and *Tenbila*—are female names. Land cannot be sold, since land existed before humans appeared. It nourished ancestors, it will nourish descendants, and it is the resting place for all people after death.

The land belongs to the group that lives on it, and each family has a portion of land to farm and cultivate. It is not normally sold to people. It belongs to them because of their family membership, and as long as that family is numerous and in need of the land, they keep it. If a family grows very small or dies out, the land goes back to the collective village. In the few cases where land is sold, religious and social ceremonies accompany the act: When the Kikuyu bought land from the Ndorobo, they performed a ceremony adopting the Ndorobo into their family.

Farming is great and important work. Among the people of Dahomey, even the King used to take part in farm labor, though symbolically. Farming is not considered inferior to town life: The people who live in the Malian towns of Bamako and Djenne believe that working the soil is a truly noble profession. The pride of farming is pride in the land and its many many crops. In West Africa, farmers cultivate rice, cotton, squash, yams, sorghum, millet, and the New World maize, manioc, sweet potatoes, and peanuts. South African farmers grow maize, bananas, and a variety of fruits and nuts. Along the river valleys, East Africans cultivate plantains, millet, maize, sorghum, and manioc, as well as rice.

African farmers understand their land as hunters understand the forest and herders the veld. Certain seeds were developed for certain areas. A farmer can tell what time to plant a crop by looking at certain stars, or counting moons, or studying the flowering of a certain tree or shrub. This understanding has existed for centuries.

The extended family—husbands and wives, sons and their wives—naturally farm together. The men usually cut down the trees, clear the land, and till the soil, while the women and children plant, weed, and harvest the crops. The Mossi extended family works together as a unit during the morning, and in the afternoon, individual men, women, and even children cultivate their own small fields. In Nigeria, among the Igbo and the Hausa, the household head gives out land to his family members; among the Bemba of Zambia each husband prepares a garden for his wife to cultivate. Farming often involves the whole village. People gather in large groups—groups of ten or more friends—for cultivating. The one who called them together feeds them and entertains them when the work is done. They have a kind of harvesting or planting bee. Dahomey has a cooperative organization called the *Dopkwe*, which gathers as a group to help each member hoe, plant, or harvest. The Jukun and the Nupe of Nigeria have the *Egbe*, an association that produces extra food or helps a family that has too much land to cultivate.

Family heads store their crops in granaries. From this supply every family is fed. Women make extra dishes for their children with the grain and vegetables from their own gardens and fields. Husbands and wives sell their produce in the market, and purchase gifts for their families. In the large kingdoms such as the Ankole of Uganda and the Lozi of Zambia, serfs or slaves (victims of war) produced food to feed the royal family and their guests.

When the crops are good and the land kind, life is full of peace, plenty, and comfort. A traditional Nigerian Yoruba poem exclaims,

> What a day, when the morning air does not resound
>   with the pounding of yams!
> What a day when I listened in vain to hear them sift the
>   flour!
> When the frying pots do not simmer with the fricassee
>   of rabbits and birds.
> What a day when the expert wakes up under the shadow
>   of starvation!

And yet, farming was not always the only occupation in African societies. Most of them also had craftsmen who manufactured their goods for sale in the markets or for use by the neighbors. In some societies, craftsmanship was a casual occupation; farming, the chief one. And because people needed tools with which to farm, ironsmiths always had work to do.

The metalsmith in Africa was deeply respected and often feared. Dealing with fire in his forge and hearth, he had a kind of supernatural magic. What couldn't the smithy transform? Iron could become a hoe, a knife, or an arrow; it could also become a death-dealing sword or spear. And when the smithy worked with gold, bending it into a necklace or a ring—for a present, perhaps—was he not, as the writer Camara Laye, son of a smithy, asks, "invoking the genies of fire and gold, of fire and wind, of wind blown by the blast-pipes of the forge, of fire born of wind, of gold married to fire"? Smithing was a powerful craft, done only by certain families, who sometimes married only among themselves, preserving their special craft within one family.

In the larger African kingdoms, the smiths were only part of a great number of craftsmen. Among the Mossi of Upper Volta, the Buganda of Uganda, the Nupe, Beni, and the Yoruba and Hausa of Nigeria, crafts developed so that they became almost (but not entirely) removed from agriculture. There were ironworkers, carpenters, canoe builders, leatherworkers, slippermakers, and masons. There was goldwork and elaborate sculpture. There were bronzes and carved elephant tusks. Bark cloth was made, as well as drums and musical instruments. Cloth was tie dyed, and metal was worked into many shapes. Both men and women worked, though not in the same crafts. In some societies men did the smithing and women the potting. In almost every group, women make yarn, but it is the men who are most often found as weavers.

Some crafts and craftsmen, such as the musicians in the Sudan, did not have high prestige. They often begged for money. Other craftsmen were aristocrats of a sort, employed and protected by the King or chiefs. The goldsmiths in Ashanti and the ivory carvers in Benin both had special tasks and privileges. In Buganda, the smiths of the *Nvubu* or Hippopotamus family always made the royal shields, bracelets, anklets, and ornaments. The smiths of the *Ente* or Cow family made the weapons and the farming instruments for the royal household. Every three months, the palace called in twenty men to work as smiths, each producing seven spears, twenty hoes, twenty-five polished knives, eighty peeling knives, fifteen adzes, seven awls, forty small needles, and thirty large needles. For their efforts they enjoyed free land, no taxation, and exemption from any other kind of work.

Some craftsmen organized into guilds, and these guilds gradually became more powerful and more independent. They were often granted monopolies by the rulers; they began to arrange their members' marriages and livelihood.

African people exchange goods in many ways. In Ruanda, where the Batwa, Tutsi, and Hutu live, most goods are exchanged by barter: meat and honey for arrows, vegetable food, and milk. The !Kung of the Kalahari exchange meat and ostrich feathers with the Tswana people for grain and arrows. But manufactured goods, agricultural products, cattle, and the gathered fruits of most African peoples come together in innumerable markets. Markets are more than places where people barter goods and sell them for money consisting of iron bars, hoes, cloth, bracelets, and cowrie shells. Markets are a kind of melting pot, where people from different villages, districts, kingdoms, and regions meet. The people bring messages, they look for friends and marriage partners; they hope to make enough money to buy gifts for their families.

The larger markets spread through West Africa, Central Africa, and Zaire—though not as much as through East Africa—are hives of activity. They may be held in cycles every four, five, eight, or sixteen days, depending upon the society. In each district or region, different villages start their market cycles on different days, and so there is always a market, somewhere, to go to. In some large towns these go on in the day, in some at night. One village market may specialize in pots, another in good maize, a third in exceptional iron hoes. Each market has its particular set of customs, its own structure, with people—wives, husbands, and children—sitting in areas according to what they are selling. The Mossi market is highly organized, with rings, from the outermost to the central portion. People sit in each ring according to where they come from; in the outside ring, nothing is sold; in the next, perhaps meat, then cloth, then leather goods, then pots.

Small or large, the markets link many parts of Africa. Traders and traveling merchants or *caravaners* visit market after market, selling goods that local people want and purchasing goods that people eight villages away might have use for. People travel great distances to get to markets; messages can be carried across several provinces. The King

Throughout Africa, the marketplace is not only the place where people buy and sell goods, but it is also a place where people socialize, exchange information, and meet new friends.

or chief can collect taxes in the marketplace. New crafts can be discovered and sampled. And, with so many people from so many different places, the market can be dangerous—fights can break out, old family and village feuds rekindle. Markets often have ritual shrines, where people give offerings to the local spirits, asking for the peace of the market. The Mossi have their market near the ruler's home, so that he may settle fights and feuds; the Yoruba have a Mother of the Market, who is the final judge of all conflicts.

Market days may bring great fortune to people. A family head, selling some of the produce from his village may, with his returns, be able to purchase cattle for a much-needed bride token, or help a needy friend. A woman may help her brother, or buy food and trinkets for her children. No one is limited by what a neighbor or friend or even a relative is doing in the market; yet, they do not compete viciously with each other. The market is the place where one can help himself. Group work such as farming, hunting, or herding satisfies the group, and the market satisfies each individual's personal desires. The private and the public; the social and the economic and the religious: All of these factors, Africans believe, should come together for a good life. All, separately and joined, are necessary for a good life, and the demands of one should not conflict with the demands of the others.

4

KINSHIP AND MARRIAGE

"The lizard and the crocodile have the same stomach—if one eats, the other should also get a morsel," goes a Fanti proverb. These people of Ghana say that the lizard and the crocodile are members of the same large family, and so one cannot live comfortably and let the other starve. African children learn, as they grow up living among their kin, that a long but orderly chain binds them to their parents, grandparents, sisters, brothers, uncles, cousins, and ancestors. Each African child learns to trace his or her descent through male ancestors, or through female ones, or sometimes through both.

African children grow up in villages or in sections (wards) of their villages, with their patrilineal or matrilineal relatives. In patrilineages, all of the village or ward men are brothers of the child's father or grandfather. They may be descendants of his great-grandfather. The child calls all of these men father, and he calls and treats his playmates as brothers and sisters. When he becomes an adult, his own children and those of his brothers are his sons and daughters. In a matrilineage, the village is inhabited by women, their husbands, their daughters, and the husbands of their daughters. And so the growing children have a village filled with "mothers" of all ages.

The terms that Africans use for their relatives sometimes puzzle visitors, but they are easy for people who value the fine network of relationships that passes from generation to generation. For example, Mossi children not only call their father's brother father; they call all of the men in mother's brother's village mother's brother. They call all of the sisters of these men mother. Is not their own mother one of these women? And since mother's brother's sons and daughters live in that village, they call them mother's brother and mother. However, when a girl grows up and leaves that village, her children, like the children of all "mothers," are called sister and brother, and their children are called son and daughter.

There is a steadiness to this life with one's kin, but there is continual movement too. African women move quite often. Growing up with their parents in the village of their birth, they then leave for another village when they marry. In some societies every mother in every village once lived in another place, and belongs not only to her husband's family, but to her father's as well. And these two centers of her family life are bound together through her sons and her brothers.

Mother's brother (uncle) is special in the life of many young African boys. For instance, the Bathonga of Mozambique call him "male mother." The uncle is the boy's confidant and his protector. His love for the boy is mixed with sadness. After all, his sister left her family to be married. She made a journey from her original home, and was given away to strangers. It could not have been otherwise. For Africans do not marry members of their own families, and to marry outside of one's family, one must usually leave the village. Still, the family line is broken with this departure. A lineage that sends its daughters away gives children to another lineage. Had the girl been a boy, she would have stayed at home, her children with her. Thus her children, her sons particularly, represent a lost possibility. Nevertheless, they have a few rights in the family that might have been their own. Mother's brother lets the child take livestock from his home, and his wife gives the child food. When the child is in trouble with his own family, he goes to mother's brother, and always finds support. That family's ancestors know that the boy was lost to them, and they would say, "Our daughter's son has come back to us. Had she been a man, she would have been here, and he would not have had to go away. But you, the living, gave her away and sent her to live among strangers. They don't treat her son well; he has come back. Protect him!"

The boy, in turn, cares for his mother's family, and helps protect their lineage. If mother's brother treats his wife badly, she can speak of it to the boy, saying, "What kind of a person is your mother's brother? Doesn't he know how to treat a wife? Have you seen your mother's brother lately? Have you seen him in the marketplace, drinking up all his money? Have you not seen him running around with the women? Have you not heard that your mother's brother mistreats his wives? What kind of person is your mother's brother?

And if the wife herself acts badly, showing too little concern for her children perhaps, the boy must speak to her, never offending or chastising her directly, but hiding his advice to her in joking remarks.

But if a boy can take many liberties with his mother's brother, he must often be quite careful with his father's sister. After all, she is a member of his own father's family, and had she been a man, she would be called father. She is, in fact, a female father, and demands a boy's good behavior as firmly as does his father. She is very much concerned with the reputation of her family. And yet, the children of these female fathers are born away from the village, are really the children of a strange man, and are simply called cousins.

African grandparents are deeply bound to their grandchildren. As we have already said, some children are named after their grandparents, and there is a strong belief that grandparent and grandchild are part of the same cycle of nature, one's life preparing to end as the other begins and starts to grow. Often, Africans make no distinction between grandfather and grandmother, calling them simply grandparents, as the young ones are called grandchildren.

In some matrilineal societies, the sons live and work in both their father's village and their mother's brother's village. Among the Ashanti of Ghana, when a woman marries, she remains with her own family, merely visiting her husband until their first child is born. Only then does she move to her husband's village, where her son, should she have one, is taught and reared until he is grown and ready to cultivate his own land. Once ready, he returns to his mother's village, where his family rights are, and there he claims the land that awaits him. By this time his mother too may have returned home, having finished bearing children. In Zambia, when a Bemba girl marries, she does not leave her parents and her home village; she brings her husband there. The couple remain in the village, with their children, until her father dies. Then they move, following the husband back to his mother's village.

Family and extended family are the center of African life, and it is marriage and children that see that it continues. Marriages are not just the union of two people. They are the uniting of two families, the creating of bonds between two villages. Marriage is not totally separated from what we call romantic love, but such love is never seen as the foundation for marriage. Marriage is too serious a matter, and too far-reaching a one to be left entirely to two young people. There are certain considerations. For one thing, no man or woman may marry anyone related to him or her in the same line as far back as five generations. A girl may be encouraged to marry her father's sister's son; a boy may be urged to court his mother's brother's daughter, but these persons are not "family" in patrilineal societies.

Generally, marriages are arranged. A man may see a good friend's pregnant wife in the marketplace, and ask her politely if his son may marry her child, should it be a girl. Flattered and pleased, the prospective father may agree to the match, with equal politeness. In the Sudan and Kenya, Nuer and Kikuyu youth may themselves make the first move. When a boy sees a girl he likes, he visits her, talks with her whenever he can, assures himself that she likes him too, and then invites the families to make the plans.

Once a marriage is made, it is sealed and celebrated with a bride token. In Europe, a girl was expected to take a dowry or gift to her husband; in Africa, the bridegroom and his relatives offer gifts to the bride's family. A bride token is not a single extravagant gift, marking the day of the marriage; it is the token of a long-lasting relationship, the mark of a new concern between families. The Upper Volta Mossi engage in a long series of gifts and services. The final and greatest gift is the bride herself, and the children she will bear. The gift-giving is a long, ceremonious process. First, the Mossi must like the prospective bridegroom. They must like his character and consider him a friend. Once he is accepted as a friend, the two families begin to feast together, and help each other in work. Eventually, a Mossi friend of the suitor feels that the time to speak has come, and so he approaches the senior elder of the group—a father or uncle—and exchanges well-chosen words with him. "Father," he says, "the people of my friend's village have been very nice to us. You remember, when we were digging a well, they came. You remember, when uncle died, they brought us food. You remember, when I was going to Kumasi, I borrowed a donkey. What can we give these people to show our appreciation?" The elder says, "Let us give them a piece of cloth." "Cloth," says the friend; "that's good, but cloth wears thin." "Well," says the elder, "let us give them food then." "Ah, yes," replies the friend thoughtfully, "but food fills once, and then the next day you're hungry." "Well," suggests the elder, "I do have a silver bracelet in my hut—what about that?" "Silver," says the friend. "Silver lasts a long time, but have you seen a silver bracelet that is very old? It becomes very thin, and it may get lost—you may never find it." "Well," says the elder at last, "what can we give him that will last as long as human beings exist in the world?" "Let us," says the friend, "give him a little thing to cook his food and bring water for him."

The expectant bridegroom is then told by his friend that he can expect an important visit very soon. He goes home and eagerly reports to his kin that his friends are coming to see him, and each morning he and his relatives get up to look down the path leading to the village. At last the visitors arrive; the bride-to-be's family are fed well, then return home. They visit again, and again, and finally the day comes when the sought-after announcement of marriage is made.

The announcement of a coming marriage by African families marks the start of handing over the bride token, or the exchange of gifts. Among the Nkundu of Zaire, through the marriage broker or *ndanga*, the future husband first presents the *ikula*: a knife, two copper rings, or an arrow. If the woman and her kin accept the *ikula*, the betrothal is official. If the family refuses but the young woman agrees, she may run off with man and wait with him until her family agrees. But when all are agreed and the *ikula* is accepted, the marriage, or *tradition* of the bride, may take place. Many gifts are given at the marriage, each one having a meaning beyond its use. The *ndanga* is offered to the bride's father: a large knife, followed by five to ten copper bracelets; it is a sign that the husband is now responsible for accidents that might befall the woman. Next the husband offers the *walo*, the most important present: many metal objects; copper bracelets, bones, spears, and arrows, strings of pearls, livestock, and other valuable gifts. Now the marriage has been completed. The ceremony turns to celebration. More grain and cattle and fruits go to the husband's family; special gifts go to the bride's mother. All members of both families join in the gift-giving celebration. If the groom's cousin offered a cow to the bride's family, that cow goes to the bride's cousin; the uncle who gave grain receives grain in turn. In return, the bride's family offers her husband's family gifts called the *nkomi*: pots, calabashes, mats, salt, livestock, and the like, which they may share with his wife. Last, the husband offers the *busongo*—a collection of copper rings—and the couple travel to their new village to begin life together.

But the bride is leaving her family, and so no marriage is without sadness. Her family cannot hide their grief; they can only make it a part of the ceremony, and thus ease it. In Botswana, on the day set for the marriage, the young men of the bridegroom's family drive the cattle to be given as the bride token to the bride's home. As they draw near, the women of the bride's party gather in front of the entrance to the corral. The men try to drive the cattle into the corral; the women run toward them fiercely, shouting, waving sticks, and driving the cattle across the field.

The men chase after the cattle, and gather them once more; the women, with new force, drive them away. At last their protests fade, and, reluctantly, they allow the men to drive the animals into the corral, then allowing the groom to take the bride away. The bride's going has been accepted by them, and the marriage will take place. And still, even after the marriage, all is not settled. The bride must be feasted and feted and persuaded by her new family's kindness to remain with them. The Jie people of Uganda sing and dance for the bride, and still she often returns to her mother's home, having to be drawn back again, enticed into settling down as a wife.

Once a wife, the bride will be very busy. She cleans and cooks for her husband steadily—if she is his only wife. For a certain time she performs these duties if she is one of several wives. Masai women of Kenya tend the cattle they receive upon marrying, and they pass these cattle on to their sons. Kikuyu women work in the fields, growing their own crops to feed their children and sell in the market. Yoruba women in Nigeria do not farm; they trade in the large, busy marketplaces.

Marriage is precious to Africans. Every family wants the couples living among them to stay together happily, working and raising children. Wives must be diplomatic with their husband's parents. Sometimes, living in the same house as her father-in-law, a woman avoids speaking to him directly at any time. She is dependent upon her husband, and that makes her twice as dependent upon her husband's father. If she is ill-treated by her husband, she

*Masai women tend the cattle they receive as dowry from their hus-
bands. The cattle are then passed on to their sons.*

often complains to his uncle or his brothers, but her real and deep bond to her husband's family is through her children. In some homes she is called only "child's mother."

Conflicts arise in some African families. Life is not always as one wants, and harmony is not always possible. If two people simply cannot live together, they are divorced, though seldom "officially." The political system of African societies has no part in a marriage. Because it was made between two families, the government has no part in the divorce, unless it is called upon to settle quarrels about the disposition of the bride token. In some societies the token is returned to the husband's family; in others—if children have been born—it is not. The woman returns to her family; the man remains with his family. Perhaps both will marry again.

At its best, though, marriage in Africa is a joining together of two people and two families; a celebration of the family looking back to the ancestors and forward to the descendants. A West African poet, C. Enitan Brown, speaks lovingly of "marriage cordiality":

> Flowers of the field are pleasant to watch,
> Oh! It is just enough to compare the sight
> Along that broad street to flowers on the march
> As blooming flowers attract butterflies in flight . . .
> On that day of marriage cordiality.

5

POLITICS AND SOCIETY

"If Otsibo says he can do something, then he does it with his followers," say the Fanti of Ghana, speaking of chiefs and the people they govern. People must work together, whether their task is to harvest the season's crops, or to judge a man who has stolen a neighbor's cattle, or to prepare for a marriage feast and celebration. Law and order are not strict systems that force people to blindly obey certain orders; they are a collection of actions and decisions and beliefs that bind people together and help them live peacefully with themselves and with each other.

Different African societies join and organize the lives of their people in different ways. Igbo, Tonga, Kikuyu, and Tiv societies pass on most decisions and laws through family elders. The power and prestige of these elders is great among people who belong to the same large family and who can trace their ancestry back to a common man or woman, for the elders are closest in age and wisdom to the ancestors. Ancestors are not just legends; people remember them and look to them for protection. Village elders have lived long and learned from their own elders; they have seen many things. "If your grandmother tells you to do something, do not tell her that you are going to find out from your mother," say the Fanti, "for who brought forth your mother?" And so as the elders control the crops or the cattle, and organize the work teams, they also appeal to the ancestors for justice and wisdom. Ancestors guard communities. It is they who give good crops and help the children to grow, and guard against diseases. And so the elders who keep order among their descendants do not speak for or from themselves; they look to and speak the wisdom of those who have passed beyond life.

In societies where the elders govern, if a man or woman steals, or fights bitterly with a friend or relative, or, far worse, commits murder, the crime is believed to be a crime against the community and against the ancestors. The crime is against the spirit of what is just and fair. A crime is a moral wrong, and its punishment is moral too. The elders of the Karamojong people of Kenya punish wrongdoers with curses. These curses bring early death, or blight crops, or make women unable to bear children. The wrongdoer has set himself apart from friends, relatives, and neighbors, and must recognize the wrong and plead for forgiveness: "Father, father," the unhappy person cries to the judging elder, "help me, help me. Leave me alone. I will not do these things again, truly. I will not repeat them." He does not plead falsely, and he is not punished needlessly. The elder forgives, saying, "Very well. Have you believed?" "I have," replies the wrongdoer. "Do you still argue?" "No," says the wrongdoer, "I have believed." He has believed in a way of life, an order and peace larger and more important than the satisfaction his deed has given. He has believed, and must again believe in, a certain way of life.

In Nigeria, the Igbo elders, or *okparas*, call upon the ancestor, the *ndichie*, and upon religious force to help the offender see the wrongness of his misdeed. They strike the earth, the goddess Ale, with the *ofo* sacred rod. The power of the earth, which gives life and shelters the dead, can be terrible. To rebel against the power of Ale is to court personal disaster and invite trouble and sorrow for the whole community.

Crimes such as theft, cheating, and violence do not hurt only the victim, and the wrong is not just the wrongdoer's. To the ancestors who judge, such a crime affects everyone. Among the Tonga of Zambia and Mozambique, suicide, or a man beating his sister or uncle, may bring down *malweza*, or punishment for the whole group. Peace can only be made through a special ceremony; every member of the group must atone and ask forgiveness. The lives of men and women living together in a society are joined together for both good and evil—"The lizard and the crocodile have the same stomach—if one eats, the other should also get a morsel"—and if one eats a poisoned morsel, the other too will become sick. Americans too have such a proverb: "One bad apple spoils the whole barrel."

Since wrongdoing touches a person's neighbors and relatives, it is often they who must punish the wrong. The age sets of men and women often take charge of punishing an offending member. The elder members of an Igbo or

Kikuyu age set judge an argument between two people, decide which one was wrong, and agree upon a certain punishment. They then order the offender's age set members to carry out that punishment. Among the Kpelle in Liberia and the Mende in Sierra Leone, the age set of young women protects each other from wrong and acts together to punish all outside offenders. When they become young wives, they act together. Perhaps a careless husband has neglected his wife, or forgotten to cut a much-needed path from her garden to the village. The wife's complaint becomes the complaint of her sisters in the age set, and they punish all of their husbands for the folly of one, refusing to cook, or refusing to stay with them. But they punish each other as well. If a woman is flighty and silly, that behavior reflects badly on all the women. The members of her age set may gather outside of her window, singing of her foolishness, declaring it to all who can hear, and insisting that she change her ways.

Secret societies, like the Ekpe or Leopard Society of the Igbo, and the Poro Society of the Mende, also take charge of judging and correcting the actions of their members. The Ekpe has the richest and most successful Igbo men, and they do not care to embarrass and shame one of their own publicly. So they visit the wrongdoer after dark, masked and representing the ancestors. Ancestors are beyond pettiness and personal anger; they pass fair judgment. A man is not humiliated by accepting chastisement from an ancestor; he would be if forced to accept it from a kinsman. He will not hold grudges, or think that a neighbor has judged him unfairly or cruelly; the wrong can be forgotten in due time, and the proper harmony and friendship can continue.

Most African societies have courts; they judge the wrongdoer whose crime threatens the peace of the whole community. The wrongdoer must be brought before the group, condemned by it, and, after making peace, be content to live once more by its customs and traditions. The Luo and the Kikuyu involve every family and every man in the village in lawsuits. The Igbo summon the *amala oha* or general assembly, title-making groups, and a priestly association called the Dibia, secret societies, the oracles, and the age grade associations. These groups are all a part of the fabric of village life, and they must join forces to reweave that fabric. The men of title and wealth are the leaders. Their status, power, and influence have come about through good sense and wisdom.

The dispute may be over a piece of land; every villager discusses the matter. When the discussion has ended, the leaders of each lineage retire for *izuzu* consultation; only those wise enough to see all points of view and find a compromise can participate in *izuzu*. After *izuzu*, a spokesman, chosen because he talks strongly and clearly, announces the decision. But his is not the last say, for however great his wisdom, it does not place him beyond reproach. The decision may be accepted, or it may be rejected with angry shouts. The majority wins, and the decision of the assembly-at-large is the final decision; it is the group, not a few leaders, who must be satisfied.

Still, much as African societies try to solve cases by

When a member of an African society commits a crime, he is judged
by a court, made up of the leaders of the community.

mediation, it is not always easy to persuade two people fighting bitterly to accept the judgment of others— especially if there are no strong rulers. A more important person must be summoned as authority. The Nuer of the Sudan call on a religious leader called the Leopard-skin Chief. If one Nuer murders another, he goes to the Leopard-skin Chief, and the chief offers him sanctuary until the victim's kinsmen have calmed themselves. The victim's relatives go to the murderer's relatives for restitution; the murderer's family makes sacrifices and offers cattle— as a bride token (if the victim was married) for a woman whose children bear the dead man's name.

When cases go to African courts, the judge or judges, like the general assembly in villages, must do all that is necessary to restore harmony as well as pass out punishment. They examine every case in detail, searching for the reasons behind the crime or the dispute. They trust their senses and their perceptions rather than court precedents because, they insist, no two cases are ever really alike. Their courts are not places for pronouncing people antisocial; they are places for helping people to become social once more, and because they judge, they are not superior people, they are members of the community who deserve respect only as long as they judge honestly and fairly.

People with power, be they judges, elders, Kings, or chiefs, must use it wisely, for the good of those they govern. "If Otsibo says he can do something," says an African proverb, "then he does it with his followers."

Kingship and sovereignty—the ruling of one person by another—is not a simple matter, nor a state to be taken

for granted, like the changing of the seasons, or the growing up of children. A King does not rule by accident or
chance; he must possess the right to rule, and he engages
forces greater than human wishes to give him that right.
Yoruba people believe that all their Kings are descendants of Oduduwa, the earth's creator. The primeval god
Olodumare, who ruled the sky, gave Oduduwa the right
to own and to rule the earth. Oduduwa then made his
sixteen sons the earth's rulers, and from these sons came
the rightful Yoruba rulers. The Mossi of Upper Volta do
not believe that their Kings descend directly from God,
nor from his sons. But it was God, they insist, who gave
men the *Nam*, that special power that lets a simple man
rule other men.

Yet wars, and marriage, and luck can create Kings too.
The Tutsi of Ruanda and Burundi were conquerors, and
so gained the right to rule; likewise did Sundiata, a King
of ancient Mali, and Chaka, King of the Zulus. African
Kings had to be ready for wars, and they organized armies
to attack their enemies or to defend their territories. But
Africans, like other people, do not like to admit that they
make wars or seize land by force. Thus, the people of
Benin claim that they asked Oduduwa, renowned King of
the Yoruba, for a son to govern them. The young prince
who came to Benin married a daughter of the land, and
their child grew up to become Benin's ruler. The Alur of
Uganda say that, plagued by drought and dry seasons,
they sought the help of certain important rain-makers.
They came to their aid, brought rain as they had promised,
and became rulers.

The African King is special, whether the ancient Egyptian Pharaoh or the more contemporary Asantehene of the Ashanti in Ghana. He has a touch of divinity; he is linked to the ancestors and to the gods of the people he rules. Many African peoples respected this divinity by veiling the King; he could not be seen by common people. He ate alone. When he coughed, courtiers clapped to hide the sound. When people approached him to make requests, they removed their shoes, touched the ground with their elbows, and poured dust over their heads. In Mali, centuries ago, the King or sultan held audiences when the sun rose. He entered dressed in a golden skullcap and velvety red tunic. He was preceded by musicians with gold and silver guitars, and followed by three hundred armed slaves. He walked slowly and majestically to his *pampe* and took his seat, to the sound of trumpets, drums, and bugles. Then the audiences began.

Ceremonies proclaim and celebrate the King's descent from the chosen ones of God. Among the Shilluk people of the Sudan, each King must battle, at a chosen spot, Nyerkang, the grandfather of all men, and the first ruler chosen by God. "There is no one above thee, thou God," pray the Shilluk.

Thou becamest the grandfather of Nyerkango.
It is thou, Nyerkango, who walkest with God. . . .
If famine comes, is it not given by Thee? . . .
Thou God, and thou who becamest Nyerkango, and thy son Bak.
But the soul of man, is it not thine own? . . .

The Shilluk, like the ancient Egyptians, divide their

land into two parts, which are joined again when the King is elected. At the ceremony, an effigy of Nyerkang is brought from northern Shilluk land. It is said that Nyerkang disappeared there during a dance. There is a mock fight between the new King and Nyerkang: The King first retreats, then is captured by Nyerkang, and at last triumphs by seizing a small girl from the ancient ruler. This girl represents Nyerkang's wife, and so the gesture means that the new King may now take his place as ruler.

Since most African Kings descended from ancestors who were either divine or chosen by divinities, their descendants continue to have divine qualities. The King of the Shilluk is not supposed to die. When a Mossi King dies, his eldest daughter dresses in his clothing and becomes the symbolic King through the funeral. Then, as the new King is chosen, a *kourita*, or young prince, is given the dead King's clothing, sword, and youngest wife. The *kourita* is then sent away from the palace. He is never to be seen by the new King, for he represents the old King, gone forever.

Yet, being a divine symbol of his people often placed heavy burdens on African Kings. For his kingdom to be peaceful and prosperous, the King was supposed to have the finest qualities of men. He should be generous, clever, strong, devoted, and brave. A man ordained a god should have the goodness of a god. A sick or evil King brings decay to the land and to the people. Kings have been asked to kill themselves for the good of the realm, and it was not expected that they would refuse. No words were spoken, and in ancient times, among the Yoruba, the unfortunate ruler was given parrot eggs as a sign. This was royal suicide; a King could also be destooled by his ministers, or defeated in an uprising, led by a young, ambitious kinsman. Protest could be simple and peaceful too. Kings were custodians of the land, not owners. A group of people displeased with their King needed only to leave his land and settle someplace else. Once a King lost his people, he lost his power to rule; he was no longer King.

African Kings were often subject to very specific injunctions from their people. The Ashanti King was always told that there were certain things he could not do. He could not reveal the genealogies of his people; he was warned not to treat them as slaves, or take their crops for his own use. He was given these commands by a group of elders (a kind of electoral college), and important kingdom officials watched his actions carefully. These officials were instructed to:

> Tell him that
> We do not wish greediness
> We do not wish that he should curse us
> We do not wish that his ears should be hard of hearing
> We do not wish that he should call people fools
> We do not wish that he should act on his own initiative
> We do not wish things done as in Kumasi
> We do not wish that it should ever be said,
>   "I have no time, have no time."
> We do not wish personal abuse
> We do not wish personal violence.

A King would be foolish to imagine that his people could not live and conduct their affairs perfectly well with-

*The power of an Ashanti King was controlled by a council of elders,
who made sure the King did not abuse his followers.*

out him. He rules from the capital of his land, surrounded
by ministers: These often include a Prime Minister, a
Minister of War, a Minister of Protocol, a Minister of
Food Resources, and a Finance Minister. Each province
in his kingdom has chiefs; so does each district and village.
In the villages and village wards, it is the elders and family
heads, as we have seen, who govern in day-to-day life. None
forget the King who rules them—after all, certain families
are making tools for him, and jewelry; some grain and
vegetables go to him regularly; certain fruit trees and
ponds belong to him exclusively. The King likes to see that
many of the province and district chiefs are his family
members. When a new King is elected, he sends his own
sons and brothers out to the provinces, and the people
there then send away the old chiefs, since they belong to
the old order. Yet, the new rulers never shatter the past
order entirely, for order is not consistent with sudden,
harsh changes. Each King's rule is joined to those before him, and with those that will follow; the province
chiefs may all be his relatives, but some of the district
chiefs may be distant relations of the old King, and some
of the village chiefs and elders might be kinsmen of the
King who ruled fifty years before.

Life for most Africans—even those who live in large
states—centers around their villages and communities, but
they are always aware of the larger worlds of district, province, and kingdom. Disputes and crimes are settled first
among families, but if they are not settled to everyone's
satisfaction, they are taken to the village chief, then to the
district chief, then to the province chief, and finally to the

King himself. The King's court is a kind of Supreme Court, and he is expected to be the wisest of judges. The King's wives too must watch over the affairs of the kingdom, for it is they, or the King's mother, who often handle the cases of many women. Sometimes neither the chiefs nor the King can take action unless the royal women have first dealt with the complaint of a woman. Still, this power is an obligation, not a force to be held over the people's heads. Kings do not declare their glory in making the "right" decision; they speak in the proverbs of the people, giving them explanations and philosophy from a common fund of wisdom. In some African societies, Kings speak through a group of interpreters, who explain his words and decisions to the people. Among the Bavenda of South Africa, the King's judgments, and their errors, were noted by a kind of court jester who was free to criticize the King.

African life joins the one to the many: The King cannot rule without the chiefs; the chiefs cannot rule without the elders; the elders cannot govern without the family; and the family cannot thrive without its members. The whole is only the sum of its parts. "Though the coconut tree is smooth," goes an African proverb, "the palm-nut tree is King." And the palm-nut tree, because of its many life-giving products, is the symbol of the people.

6

AFRICAN RELIGION

How was the earth made? How did men and women come to be on earth? Is there a God, and are there unseen forces, stronger than men and women? How do people live—by what morals?—and how do they face unhappiness, sorrow, and misfortune? What is evil? All people ask these questions, and all people try to answer them in many different ways: finding answers they believe in, and creating legends, laws, and customs that strengthen these beliefs and make them easier to live by. Religion helps many people to understand the world more clearly, and helps them live with some feeling of continuity and order.

Most peoples believe in a God, a Supreme Being who sees and knows all, who created the world, and the people, plants, and animals that inhabit it. Africans believe in a Supreme God, whether it be the God of the Nigerian Yoruba, who sent his son Oduduwa down from the sky in a canoe to create the first people, or whether it is the God of the Fon of Dahomey, who is male and female, the male named Lisa, like the sun, and the female named Mawu, like the moon. To many central and southern African peoples who speak Bantu languages, God is the "great Muntu," a person and a force, from which all other beings and creatures come. God created the world, and in many different ways, according to myths and legends. The Dogon people of Mali say that God, or Amma, first made the sun, surrounded by rings of white copper, and the moon, surrounded with rings of red copper. Then Amma threw a lump of clay into space, and the earth was made. After this Amma became lonely, and so he joined himself to the earth, thereby creating men and women.

The Fon say that Mawu and Lisa gave birth to seven pairs of twins, who ruled over earth, sea, nature, the storm, and the rest of the universe. The Luyia of Kenya tell of Wele, who made heaven first (supporting it with pillars like a hut), then the sun, the moon, the clouds, rain, and two rainbows. Afterward, Wele made two helpers and gave them the earth to work with. Rivers, lakes, mountains, and valleys followed, and when this was done, Wele made a women, a man, and many animals.

Many Africans believe that God once lived on earth with people and animals, but left, disgusted with the mistakes, bickerings, and thoughtlessness of men and women. The Yao of Malawi claim that God, or Mulungu, once lived happily on earth with animals, but found that peace shattered when humans were created. They brought disorder, setting fires that burned the bushes to the ground, and setting traps that killed the animals. Upset, Mulungu asked the spider to spin a thread to heaven, and when it was done, he climbed all the way up and never came down again.

The Nyimang in the southern Sudan say that once the

sky, God's house, was so close to earth that it pressed down on the people, making them uncomfortable. Finally, one day, the women grew angry at having been burned because they had to keep their hands low while stirring their millet porridge. One woman lifted the stirrer angrily and pierced the sky with its top end. The clouds scattered immediately and have never come close to men and women again. The Ashanti tell the tale differently: An old woman pounded her yams daily with a mortar and pestle, and kept knocking accidentally against the divine Onyankopon. She meant no harm, of course, but he was offended and left for the sky.

—Despite the fact that God left earth, Africans believe that he still watches from afar, and that the universe he made is a good one. "God go with you," is a common African greeting, as well as "God protect you," and "God give you children." To the Zulu, God is "the one you meet everywhere," and "the one who fills everything"; he is the source of the energy and force that keeps the world and everything in it growing and changing. God is mysterious, and though he can inspire people with terror and preside over destinies that are unfortunate and unhappy, he is not needlessly cruel, and he does not play with the lives of people for his own amusement. To the Akan of Ghana, he is "the one on whom men lean and do not fall." And to the Dinka of Sudan, God is not really a "he," but a power, an activity, that contains the actions of all other beings.

For God, the Supreme Being, is not the only force in the universe; it is filled with forces: human, plant, and animal, material and non-material. These act upon each other and upon men and women continually. Earth is *Ale* to the Igbo or *Tenga* to the Mossi—God's fertile wife, who gives food to people and offers them a resting place. Shango is the Yoruba god of storms and thunder, who humbles the stubborn, wishes long life to warriors, and punishes liars. The snake is a magical creature, present when the world was made, and linked to the multicolored rainbow that joins heaven and earth. The Fon see the rainbow as a cosmic snake, its red portion male, its blue portion female. The Dogon of Mali say that snake was once joined to humans: The union of God and earth created twins named Nummo, half snake and half human, representing movement and energy in water.

Since mountains, huge trees, lakes, and rivers were made by divine beings, they are believed to have powers of their own. Water, it is believed, washes away uncleanness (a familiar Christian belief too). Water, with its plant, fish, and reptile life, is life-giving and fertile.

Perhaps one can best understand African ideas of God by saying that God is the point of a pyramid. The nature gods are on one side of the pyramid, the ancestors of men and women are on the other, and humans are in the center. The first ancestors had the first human contact with God. He did not demand that they and their descendants live only to worship the divinity, and though their actions sometimes angered God, he did not send death or evil into the world as punishment. More often, the first people invited death, unhappiness, and evil through carelessness or simply accident. The ancient Hebrews believed that the snake brought death into the world. The belief of the Kono of Sierre Leone is not too different: They say that God promised the first man and woman skins to protect them from death. He sent the skins in a bundle, carried by a dog. But the dog stopped along the way, foolishly telling the other animals of his important mission. Hearing him, the selfish snake decided that the skins were too valuable to waste on men and women; he stole the bundle and shared the skins with his relatives. And so people die, but snakes revive themselves every year by shedding their old skins.

The Mende of Sierre Leone say that a dog and a toad were sent to people with two messages from God: The dog was to say that people would not die, and the toad was to say that they would. The animals left together, but the dog grew hungry along the way and stopped to eat. The toad was the first to reach the town where people dwelt, and so the message of death was the first to be delivered.

The Ila of Zambia say that God offered the first man and woman two bags, one containing life, one death. The man and woman were dazzled by the bag that shone brightly and so they chose it; that was the bag containing death. And so death became an inescapable part of the world of human beings, and became accepted simply because there was no way to avoid it. Still, there was a compensation: All who die become spirits, and so the first ancestors joined God, as do their descendants.

The ancestors are a bridge between humans and divinities or gods, since they are, in a way, both. People were not made simply to worship God; they were made to enjoy life on earth, as all divinities from God to the river spirits, know. Ancestors help people live as they should; they remind them of their duties to one another and to the gods. People must make a living: They seek the ancestors' help. Before men and women plant and cultivate their crops, they offer grain, vegetables, or animals as sacrifices to the earth goddess. She is asked to bring forth her riches; her past generosity is invoked and praised.

The ancestors and God are given respect, and offered the sustenance that they give men and women. "Great God," say the Mossi, "great God in the sky, come and take this millet water. And your wife Tenga, come and take this water. The old ancestors of the world, come and take your water." The spirits will take the living force of the grain or the vegetable and animal, as they accept the living force of the praise offered them; the actual food does not matter.

Ancestors also care about the continuing life of their descendants, and they are appealed to when a couple want children very badly. In Burundi, a prayer to God, known as Imana, goes, "Hush, child of my mother. Imana who gave you to me, if only I could meet him I would fall on my knees and pray to him. I would pray for little babies. You came when Imana lit the fire. You came when he was in a generous mood." And if a woman suffers from barrenness, she may ask sadly, "Imana, why are you punishing me? Why have you not made me like other people? Can you not even give me one little child?"

Imana may not be punishing the barren woman; but if

he is not, why can she not have children, she asks? Perhaps she is the victim of evil magic, witchcraft, or sorcery. A sorcerer can hurt a person he or she dislikes by manipulating objects that person owned. Witches can do even greater evil: They have the power to drain the vital essence from a person—to take away one's breath of life. Witches and sorcerers cannot manipulate the ancestors or God. So anyone who fears witchcraft must protect himself or herself by praying to the ancestors to prevent harm, and restore life's proper order.

But people do not blame their troubles and sorrows only on witches or sorcerers. Often a man or woman, or a whole village suffering from misfortune, will see in this—a crop failure, or a child's death—a sign that they are not living as they should. What happens in the world around one is always tied to what happens inside one. After all, the ancestors usually protect their descendants. When they fail to, it is because they believe the descendants have forgotten them, or, in false pride, chosen to think that they no longer need spiritual help. Such a thought is always false, and very foolish, for men and women are not the center of the universe, and they are not all-powerful. And so, misfortune is bound to come.

But how does a person know just why a child has died, or a relative turned into a thief, or a crop failed? Is the culprit a sorcerer? Is illness the work of a witch, intent on doing evil, or is it the reflection of one's careless, selfish behavior? As in all religions, Africans have rituals that uncover the true source of guilt; there are priests and oracles, whose wisdom helps identify right and wrong, and makes the moral order clear again. Among the Yoruba in Nigeria and the Fon in Dahomey, the priesthood is highly organized, like Christian churches, with convents, nuns, priests, and a hierarchy of different priests for different gods. Most priests are people who feel holy and called to their work. A priest will tell a woman who wants children, or who suffers from disease, whether or not she is the victim of a sorcerer. Priests have ways of finding the cause of the trouble. They may pray for divine guidance; they may conduct special ceremonies in their villages, for the entire community. Priests in the cult of *Ifa* have sixteen palm nuts, which they move about carefully. The nuts fall into different combinations, combinations that tell the priests the character and the root of the misfortune. Priests also have mediums, who speak, from a trance, for the ancestral spirits.

A priest may be the one who mediates a test of guilt when a crime has taken place—a test that the spirits judge. They know what the criminal has done. In a lawsuit, a priest might mix a potion containing many ingredients, and give some to each person involved. They all drink, and the one who vomits (or sometimes dies) is the guilty one. Or the drink might be given to two chickens, one symbolizing the guilty person, one the innocent. The chicken that dies represents the proper judgment. Priests also submit the problem to an oracle, like the Ibini Okpade or long Ju Ju of the Igbo in Nigeria. The oracle is the final appeal, and carries a great deal of weight. People came from long distances to consult the long Ju Ju, who had a cave up a riverbank, and those who wanted advice stood in the river and stated their case.

Priests do not just tell people about the crises of good and bad fortune in their lives; they are often wise enough to foretell the future, and many try to examine and discover the final destiny of human beings on earth. But such predictions and searchings do not mean that one's future is fixed and beyond change. To Africans, destiny is changeable, and people are not playthings of the gods. The gods are not to be blamed for bad luck and evil. People, at every point in their lives, have a choice. The Igbo believe that the *chi*, or central spirit of each person, must be developed and cared for through life. If it is not, the person will not fulfill his proper destiny.

It is life, not death or afterlife, that matters in African religions. One has to die, naturally, but life is good, and God and all other divinities contribute to life. Death is not dwelt upon by African people; they do not have elaborate ideas of heaven and hell. The spirit lives after death, though, joining the ancestors, and so those who die are not sent out of the world carelessly. A burial and a funeral are the last earth rituals—the burial to dispose of the human remains, and the funeral to separate the dead one from the family. Before burial, the dead one is washed and anointed so that the limbs do not grow stiff. After neighbors and relatives have seen the body, he or she is buried.

Among the Bunyoro of Uganda, if the dead one is a father, grains of millet are put in his hand, and each child approaches to take a few grains and eat them, thus showing that the bond between father and children has been broken. Certain tasks symbolize the destruction of the household of which he was head: The central pole of the house is wrenched out of place and thrown into the courtyard; the fire is put out; the household water pots are broken. The dead one is then placed in the grave. The eldest child may look into the grave to see that the parent is well laid out; the children may sprinkle the first earth on the grave; at last the grave is filled in by friends and neighbors. Food, cowrie shells, and other objects may be left with the body, for it is hoped that the surviving soul of the dead will use them. On the day of the burial, no farming is done in the village, and after the burial, all return to the house and lament the dead one's passing. "Death has stolen him from me," the women may cry; or "He is dead, my strong buffalo, my beautiful one; he has gone; he shall not be forgotten."

After the burial, there is a funeral because no one can be at ease until proper farewell has been said to the dead one. Sometimes the funeral follows quickly after burial, and covers a period of perhaps three days for men and four days for women. No one cooks; a widow does not bathe; the mourners eat with leaves, from broken pots. Friends and relatives stay with the family, comforting them, and at the end of the period, the new heir is installed. There is a feast then, for this marks the "emerging from death." There is chanting and drumming; the family provides grain, livestock, and drink, for they are returning to society what the dead man gathered for himself during his life. The dead one's wealth is divided among his family members; the guests eat and talk; when all the food is gone, they go home. For some African societies the funeral ceremony of separating the dead from the living is then completed; for others, like the Bunyoro, there follows another two-week ceremonial period, ending only when the dead one's family visits a distant relative's home to "leave the death" there. For still other Africans the funeral could be put off for as long as a year or more. But it must be done. When all of the ceremonies have been completed, the funeral is finished and life is taken up again.

Most Africans believe that a dead one's essence survives death; that the breath of life joins the universe. After all, there is the spirit of life, coming from God, and shared by all entities—ancestors, humans, plants, and animals. Life is eternal, and it comes again and again to each family. The dead one joins the ancestors, and his essence or spirit is reborn in several people; his essence may return to his family many times, through many descendants. Such a spirit is called "the spirit that comes back to see the world," and some people believe that a spirit can come back to see the world only a certain number of times. After it has completed its turns, it joins the higher spirits. As we have seen, no spirits, divinities, or ancestors ignore the world of humans.

The arrival of early Christianity in Egypt in the first century A.D., to Ethiopia in the fourth century A.D., and later on in North Africa and Nubia introduced new religious elements into Africa. After many theological debates about the nature of Christ, the Africans insisted on their own ideas and founded Coptic Christianity. Christianity was Africanized by the Ethiopians whose Kings, especially Lalibela, built spectacular underground churches. The Ethiopians and Nubians wrote the Bible in their own

Islam is still one of the main religions in Africa. Moslems worship at the mosque.

languages, and painted Christ, the Virgin Mary, and the Apostles in their own image. Similarly, when Islam appeared in Africa in the seventh century, it, too, was Africanized and made to conform to African ideas of religion. Thus even before the western Europeans arrived with their new brand of Christianity, Africans had added Christ to their indigenous deities such as Shango, Ale, Mawu-Lisa, and Mahomet to a long line of illustrious ancestors.

7

THE ARTS IN AFRICA

It is said among the Ekoi of Nigeria that Mouse brought all stories into the world. Mouse may seem an insignificant creature, but she goes all places and sees all things. Long ago she wove story children from all she saw, and dressed them in gowns of red, white, blue, and black. They lived with her and probably would have forever, but Leopard, Sheep, and a Ninm woman had a quarrel and Sheep, while running away, crashed into the door of Mouse's house and broke it down. All of the stories and histories inside ran out, and instead of returning home to Mouse, they decided to travel up and down the world, which they do to this day.

Stories, those works of the imagination, deal with everything in heaven and earth. They are part of life, as hunting, planting, marrying, and raising a family are. Such is the African view of all art, whether it be tales, poems, music, dancing, sculpture, or painting. Each has its natural place. There are masks that express love and reverence for an ancestor; there are songs that celebrate initiation ceremonies; there are dances that offer tribute to the gods of nature. They are special and yet not apart. There are also songs that a woman may hum alone while pounding grain; small figures that decorate a home; and dances for pleasure and fun, as young men and women court each other. Formulas like "art for art's sake," "art for life's sake," and "art for politics" are not enough unless all joined together: There is almost nothing in African life that art cannot be part of.

Stories and proverbs weave in and out of the fabric of African life from childhood on. Some are lessons in moral behavior; some are tales of the beginning of the world and the origins of human beings; some tell of the animal world, others of adventures. How does it come about that some people are good-looking and others, not? How did it happen that children were first whipped? How did death come into the world? Why do the sun and moon live in the sky, and why did God leave earth? There is much to think about in these tales, whether the thinker is a young child frightened of death or a man caught between responsibilities to his wife and his mother. There was once a blind man, one is told. This man's wife, mother-in-law, and mother were also blind, and they lived together in sorrow and poverty. Finally they decided to travel away together, in search of a better place and better luck. As they traveled along the road, the man stumbled over something, and discovered he had come upon seven eyes. Right away he gave two to his wife (she was very happy) and then took two for himself. There were three left. He gave one to his wife's mother and one to his own mother. The two women stared at him, each hoping for a second eye. And he was caught. If he gave the last eye to his wife's mother, his own mother would never forgive him. But if he gave it to his mother, he would forever be ashamed and guilty before his own wife. Which way is easier, and which way is right? If this thing came to you, the man is asked, which would you choose? Family relationships are delicate and complicated: One has many obligations. Such a tale reveals them, reminds people of them, and helps to ease them.

Another tale may yield more laughter, and yet there is an underlying seriousness. How did animals get their tails? According to the Bamenda of the Cameroons, all animals were made without tails, and told by the Maker to come one day to select whatever tail suited them best. The first group of animals naturally selected the longest and best tails. The second group, though less favored, still got a good selection. The last group, the hares, got lazy and told the others to pick tails for them, and so they got the short, stubby ones that no one else would bother with. The moral is clear: If you want a thing done well, do it yourself.

Poems too express many moods. Swahili poems tell of many concerns and emotions of mankind. The poet says:

> Love is wonderfully sweet, if it meets love
> It inebriates like drinking, it rules our actions,
> It cures diseases, the lame will be able to walk,
> do not love someone who has no love; love is everywhere.

Yet love causes pains:

> Love is a poison which kills secretly
> there is no scholar and no doctor (who can cure it) it makes one
> crazy and it causes poverty.

The poet laments the fall of kingdoms, and the death that takes proud rulers and warriors.

> There were once lords and ministers of state;
> They went out with troops of soldiers.
> But the earth graves gaped for them,
> The shackles of death tied them down.

The poet expresses in a few quick words, the relation between the wisdom of men and the word of God.

> Efforts do not avert fate;
> the arts of men are of little avail;
> the written [word] does not go back even once.

Poems, tales, and stories are not just told; they are chanted, sung, and danced. The tale teller can have a chorus with him, and the listeners clapping and joining in (for all know the story). For the arts work apart *and* together in African life. Stories join song and dance; dances are often performed in masks, which are works of sculpture. What Westerners call "mixed media" and consider avant-garde is natural in African art.

Take praise singing. The praise singers of Western Africa (or *griots*) are poets, historians, heralds, and musicians. They sing the history of families, praising their noble deeds, "filling their hearts." In the days of royalty, each kingly family supported a group of praise singers. They are the keepers of history; they perform at wedding celebrations, religious ceremonies, work gatherings, and in private homes. They are renowned for the beauty of their music and singing, as well as for their mastery of history, and their weaving of it into a kind of poem.

86

Singing abounds in African life. Babies are sung to sleep with lullabies, arguments conducted in, or are settled in song, ancestors are praised, and goods are sold in the marketplace with song. Private pain can be eased with song. "We were three couples, including me, Kodio Ango," goes a Baule song of the Ivory Coast:

We were on our way to work in the city
And I lost my wife Nanama on the way
I alone have lost my wife.
To me alone such misery has happened
To me alone, Kodio, the most handsome of the three men such
     misery has happened
In vain I call for my wife
She died on the way like a chicken running
How shall I tell her mother
How shall I tell it to her, I Kodio, when it is so hard to hold
     back my own pain?

Or confusion at a new way of life, as when the Nyasa children of Malawi sing about the European newcomers:

Europeans are little children.
At the riverbank they shot an elephant.
Its blood became a canoe, and it sank;
and it sank oars and all.
I collected wild sorghum for Miss Mary.

Girls and boys flirt with each other in song, separating into two groups, the boys boasting of their strength and knowledge, the girls making fun of them.

The transition from boyhood to manhood, or girlhood to womanhood is an occasion for much singing, as well as dancing. Adangme girls in Ghana are taken into the *dipo*

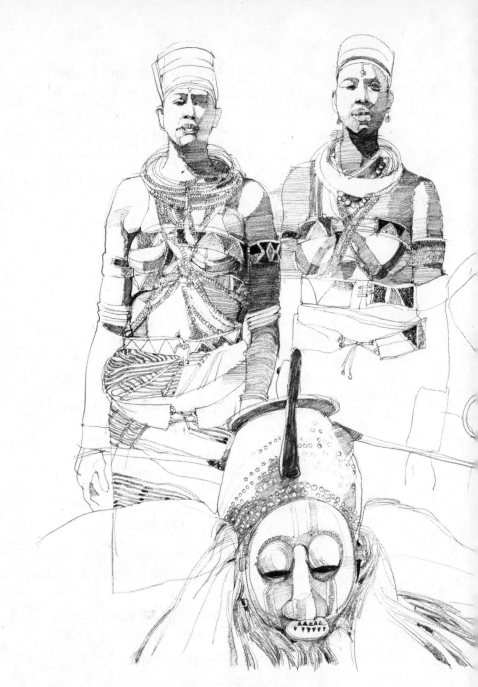

Songs and dances are often performed in masks that are works of art.
Song is another way to communicate in African life.

(initiation school) and taught the special music and dances of the ceremony, the customs and the history of their society, and mother crafts. They are put on a fattening diet so that on graduation day they will be beautiful and plump. On the day of graduation, there are feasts, singing, dancing, and drumming parties, and musical processions to the ritual places. Didinga girls in Karye learn to sing of the tasks they are taught by their mothers, such as the shaping of pottery; and young boys preparing for initiation are taught songs of courage and bravado. "Today is a great day," say Bangi boys of the Central African Republic:

> For us, the youth
> Among us no girl can be found,
> We have nothing to do with love today.
>
> Tonight our sweetheart will be alone in her house.
> Whoever lay down in the village
> Will sleep tonight in the forest
> And the beloved will cry for her lover.

And Bangi girls sing, somewhat sadly, of the leaving of old and familiar responsibilities:

> Today I am going to be an initiate,
> I shall leave the house of my mother,
> I shall no longer see
> Either my father or my brothers:
> Who then will bring them water?
> Who will prepare their meals?
> Who will sweep their house?

Voices can be used like instruments too—a different one to suit the particular song. Among the Ashanti, minstrels use a certain voice quality that they use nowhere else, to sing about ancestor chiefs. In Ghana, the hero of Akan folk tales, Ananse or Spider always speaks in a nasal voice. In Dahomey, voices imitate trumpets, when a trumpet maneuver used by King Abaka in one of his wars is praised. Often, in groups, there are separate choruses for men and women, with each singing a certain kind of music.

Instrumental music is as important in African life as vocal. Any sound is potentially musical: a bell, the pounding of a rock, sticks clattering, hands clapping, seeds inside a gourd. Instruments are made of the materials at hand: wood, horsehair, ivory and animal horns, rope, skin, fruit shells, clay, gut, or metal. There are four kinds of instruments, and within each group are many, many variations. Each can be played alone; all can be played together.

First are the *idiophones*: cowbells, clappers, stamping tubes, iron bells, clangers, castanets, thumb pianos, xylophones, and rattles made from fruit shells, strung beads, or cowries. Idiophones are used everywhere, and joined by hand-clapping, or foot-stamping, with ankle bells and buzzers on the musician's body. There are *aerophones* too, or wind instruments. Horns are made from elephant tusks, or carved from the horns of large animals: They are specially treated, and decorated. Trumpets are made out of gourd, or carved out of wood; their range is narrow. There are flutes and whistles too, carved from bamboo.

Stringed instruments (*chorophones*) are used less than the others—mostly in homes, or in combination with voices. There are lutes of many kinds: picked lutes, bowed lutes; the one-, two-, and three-stringed fiddles. There are harps and zithers—one a musical bow, played inside the mouth, or with an attached open gourd.

Finally, there are the drums, the *membranophones*, perhaps the most important group of instruments. They set and punctuate the rhythms of African music, the rhythms that can be set against each other, as many as fifteen or twenty at a time. There are kettledrums, bottle-shaped drums, hourglass drums, goblet drums, pot drums, frame drums, and gourd drums. There is a way to play each one: a stick technique, a hand and stick technique, a hand technique, fingers spread or cupped. Drums serve many purposes. They are musical, accompanying dance or song. They can be signals—calls or warnings or greetings. And, overlapping with stories and verse, they can speak. Proverbs, played on Akan drums, can be mind teasers, and there are over seventy of them.

> The path has crossed the river.
> The river has crossed the path.
> Which is the elder?
> Who made the path and found the river.
> The river is from long ago,
> From the creator of the Universe.

Messages can be sent with drums; many African languages are based on tonal differences, and the drums, often called gongs, with their varying tones, imitate those tones of the languages. Gong language is very expressive; an orphan may be described by the gongs in this way: "The child who has no father nor mother, he begs for food in the communal hut." Low-pitched gongs are the males, high-pitched the females, and the gongs too are given names, expressing the

The drum is a means of communicating in many African societies. Not only is it used as a musical instrument, but also as a form of speech.

temper or the philosophy of the village or clan that uses them. The gong of a Zaire village whose people are leaving is named "Birds do not steal from a person without food." A family mocked by others for its decreasing size calls its gong "Ears of mine, do not listen to what people say"; but a cockier family calls its gong "The male elephant waves his trunk about."

So drums are both speech and music. They are played singly or in ensemble; by themselves, or with rattles, flutes, zithers, or other instruments. They set dance rhythms; they mark the rhythm of a funeral dirge.

The variety of musical instruments matches the variety of music's use in African societies. Music is recreation—there are bands or associations that specialize in music and dance for play and amusement. Music is religious too, used when prayers to ancestors and gods are offered, used to mourn a dead relation. And it is a part of day-to-day life, as people farm, hunt, care for their children and sisters and brothers, quarrel, and joke. It is a blending of opposites: sound and sense, work and play, art and life, tradition and change.

Art too is part of the process of living. The masks, worn at initiation and public ceremonies, in secret societies, and at funerals are symbols, embodiments of forces and ancestors. They are a medium, through which justice can be meted out in a court, without human error. It is the masked rituals and dances that teach young initiates their people's history, the laws they must learn to follow, and the principles of good they must uphold as grown men and women.

It is the masks that symbolize the Igbo ancestors, those forces that watch over men and women, and mediate between them and the gods of the universe. Masks are the embodiments of supernatural beings. In the Ivory Coast, Senufo masks appear during farming ceremonies to call for rain, or ask for a good harvest. Some masks send a dead man's spirit away, when a family's period of mourning has ended. Mende woman of Sierra Leone wear helmetlike masks for their initiation ceremonies, and the Bambara of Mali have a mask that is worn to ensure good relations with the neighboring people. Masks are a way of making the supernatural natural, and the unseen seen. They can resemble humans, or they can be part human and part animal. A mask may have one nose, or three noses, or no nose at all. They are made of wood, iron, ivory, copper, gold, brass, animal skins, or hair. They are dyed, colored, carved, or engraved. In most ceremonies they are worn with costumes made from raffia or another woven material, cloth, or twine. Some masks are worn on top of the head, some over the face. The men, and sometimes women, who wear the masks and the costumes in rituals and ceremonies may hide their identities as they dance and chant, changing their voices and moving differently. And yet, even when they do not, the power of the forces they represent is not destroyed; the mask gives them a separate, independent identity.

Like music, African art is as much a part of everyday, practical living as it is of the religious and spiritual life. Africans decorate their faces or bodies with colorful powders, pastes, and paint, and take advantage of the keloid-forming characteristics of their skin to carve intricate designs on their bodies. They weave, plait, or sculpture their hair in hundreds of intricate styles. Also, both men and women enhance their beauty by shaving all the hair from their heads. Africans weave cloth, tie-dye, and make clothing from leather. Spoons, vessels, doors, and house posts are carefully and intricately carved from wood. Among the Ashanti, the stools of the Kings, Queen Mothers, and chiefs each have different designs. The Ashanti also make small figures out of brass to weigh gold, figures portraying birds, insects, plants, and animals.

Wooden figures of many sizes rest in homes and marketplaces, representing ancestors, or gods (there is a god of the marketplace, to be appealed to for keeping the peace). Ashanti women sometimes carry small figures in their clothing to ensure that their children will be well-formed —a kind of amulet. Yoruba and Dahomean families with twins may have statuettes (*ibeji*), carved to represent them. Should one twin die, the other carries a statuette, so that the dead one's spirit will not haunt the family. Women who have lost both twins wear both statuettes in their belts. There are fertility figures; there are figures to be used by diviners; there are caricatures of certain village types—a pompous official perhaps, or a missionary.

Art, music, dance, and literature cannot easily be divided up and carefully labeled in Africa. No one art form can be isolated into a single category: Sculpture joins with dance, dance with music, music with stories and proverbs. And religious art is joined to practical art, and both are art for amusement and pleasure. Take the Kalabari people of the Niger delta in Nigeria. Each Kalabari community has a men's society called Ekine, or "The Dancing People," and each society puts on a cycle of plays, from thirty to fifty. The Ekine plays or masques are dedicated to the water spirits, and ask for their help: It must, then, be a religious society. But the Ekine are also part of community government, settling cases where individuals have been wronged—debt perhaps, or insults. So perhaps the masques are meant to teach villagers a moral lesson? The masques are very beautiful, too, blending stories, dance, drumming, and singing, are wonderfully costumed, and the dancers are trained for many years. "We are here for laughing, drinking, and for the play," say the Kalabari. And that suggests that they are performing solely for pleasure and entertainment.

None are true separately; all are true together. The Kalabari myths tell of how the dancing water spirits abducted Ekineba from a delta town, and took the beautiful woman to their home beneath the creeks. But their mother grew angry and commanded them to take Ekineba back to the land of men. The spirits agreed to, but before returning, each showed Ekineba its special play, and when she returned home, she taught them to the people. These plays grew very popular, and were performed all the time, but there was one problem: The spirits had ordered that, whenever the people put on one of their plays, Ekineba must be the first to beat the drum. The people disobeyed this order three times. And so the water spirits lost patience, and took Ekineba away forever. Since that time, men have taken her as the patron goddess of the masquerade.

Each play cycle begins with the Ekine members going down in canoes to a place in the creeks known as "Beach of the Water Spirits." They call the spirits, announce that the plays are about to begin, and invite them to attend. The spirits, it is believed, return to town with the Ekine members, and with an offering and a prayer to Ekineba, the plays begin. Each play is bound up with one of the water spirits: During the play, as the masker, nimble and quick, moves with the drum rhythms, the spirit is said to walk with him and enter his legs. When the last play is over, dancers from each play join together, dancing in the morning, just before ebb tide, "Stretching the Canoe of the Water People." At ebb, they all go down to the beach known as "Pouring-out Place of the Water Spirits," take off their costumes, and bathe. And thus they send the spirits back to the creek. It seems to be a religious ceremony. And yet, these water spirits are not very important in the religious life of the Kalabari, and some are considered small-time troublemakers. The plays present life as it is rather than as it should be. The characters are often familiar, and often funny, though not always flattering: the dignified househead, the good-for-nothing aristocrat, a suspicious doctor, and a cunning liar, out to trick or deceive everyone. And the mask serves very practical purposes for its dancer: It increases his prestige, and permits him to display his wealth through lavish costumes and feasting.

And so, the Kalabari masques are a complex mixture of

human and artistic elements, a balance that teaches, entertains, and links people to the supernatural, through dancing, music, stories, and art. And African art is a balance too, a bridge that crosses from the natural world to the spiritual one, letting each exist fully on its own, but never letting them separate entirely from each other.

8

AFRICA TODAY

Today Africa is a kaleidoscope of the traditional and the modern. It is not a question of the static clashing with the moving, or even of the old against the new. For traditional Africa is the crystallization of a long, long period of change. African societies have never been static; but changes were once gradual, more easily blended with the existing way of life. Modern Africa and the changes that have created it are different, because these changes, brought about in many cases through European contact, conquest, and colonialism, haven't yet merged with the traditional cultures of Africa. Africa is in transition, still seeking ways to keep the old and use the new, and so there is conflict, confusion, determination, and, most of all, uncertainty. Where is the old path, Africans ask, and what direction is the new?

Many factors brought Africa to its present-day position at the crossroads. Arabs invaded Africa in the seventh century, and Moslem armies, traders, and clerics had an enormous effect on North Africa, the western Sudan, and East Africa until the sixteenth century. The Arabs traded for gold, wanted slaves for domestic household uses, and spread their religion (Islam) by the sword when necessary.

However, the Africans soon tamed Islam. But the strongest force to hit Africa in recent times was western Europe, with its urge to expand that began in the fifteenth century. For centuries before these Europeans had been in contact with the expanding Arab nations, and even with China, through the voyages of Marco Polo. They mastered the use of gunpowder developed in China, improved upon ships and sails from the eastern Mediterranean, and studied the philosophies and religions of Judea, Greece, and the widespread Roman Empire. They were then ready to expand, but first Portugal and Spain, which had been fighting a losing battle with the Moors, had to reconquer the Iberian peninsula. This fact of war and some curiosity about the ways of other lands led them to sail around Africa and eventually to the New World, as it was known. They had heard of a Christian King in Ethiopia—Prester John—and they set out to travel around Africa, find him, and secure his aid in defeating the Moslems, who were firmly settled in Spain and North Africa. And so Vasco da Gama sailed around the Cape of Good Hope in 1498.

The Portuguese gamble paid off very well, though in unexpected ways, for they found gold. They also found people who they seemed to feel were made for their special use, for no sooner had they landed than they ambushed and kidnaped Africans, made them captives, and took them back to Europe. Word of this human and monetary wealth spread. Columbus and the Spaniards tried to follow the Portuguese and ended up in the Americas. Other Europeans, like the British, the Dutch, the Danes, the French, and the Brandenburgers, all went to Africa. Gold seemed

The Portuguese started exploration of Africa when Vasco da Gama
sailed around the Cape of Good Hope in 1498. On the continent, they
found gold and other valuable resources.

to be everywhere—the lands of the Fanti and the Ashanti became known as the "the Gold Coast." All people and ways of life were translated into money terms for these explorers. The English minted a coin worth twenty-one shillings with gold from Africa. They called it "guinea" after a town in the western Sudan, though its own people called it Jenne. Alas for Jenne, as well as Segou and Timbuktu, the gold that the Europeans were taking from the coast could no longer add to the wealth of the rulers of these cities, the princes of Songhay. So the Moroccans, with whom the Sudanese traded, were anxious to keep on getting some of this gold and they invaded West Africa and destroyed Songhay. So the Europeans' search for gold ended the last of the three golden empires: Ghana, Mali, and Songhay.

Gold, dazzling as it was, though, was only one of the wealth-producing items that European traders and merchants found in Africa, the West Indies, North America, and South America. Sugar had possibilities, and it was a taste they had acquired from the Arabs during the Crusades. Europeans learned to like tobacco, used by the Carib people in the Antilles and the West Indies. Thus mines were needed and crops had to be grown and harvested; human labor was a must. The masses of Europeans were already deeply involved in the growing Industrial Revolution, and could not be spared. And so the Europeans turned to Africa, no longer just taking their captives back home, but exporting them to the West Indies, North America, and South America to do the basic work on which the New World Western civilization would be built. They took slaves from Senegal, from the Ivory Coast (so named for the animal tusks that were made into billiard balls and piano keys), from the Gold Coast (Ghana) and from Nigeria, soon known as the Coast of Slaves.

The Western slave trade was devastating for the peoples and cultures of Africa—much more so than the Arab slave trade had been. Now the structures of their societies were shattered, as their most able-bodied men, women, and children were taken away for use as industrial slaves. African Kings, who had used slaves as domestics in their palaces, suddenly found that they were a source of new and exciting wealth. Traders gave the Kings gin, manufactured goods, cloth, iron, glassware, and, most of all, guns; in return they surrendered their domestic servants. With the guns, many of them made war on their neighbors; these neighbors were often busy protecting themselves from the same European freebooters, who anchored offshore late at night, approached land in longboats, fired on the villages, and seized everyone in sight. Attacks from these outsiders grew; internal wars became more violent, and the stakes became much higher. African political organizations were destroyed.

Still, the Europeans were limited to the fringes of African society. For 350 years they had to settle for making bargains with the African Kings, lords, princes, and chiefs because they were not strong enough to move inland on the continent alone. Trade was rewarding, though the hot, damp environment caused many of them to die from malaria. But industrialism in their own countries was growing; successful trading demanded greater successes; and

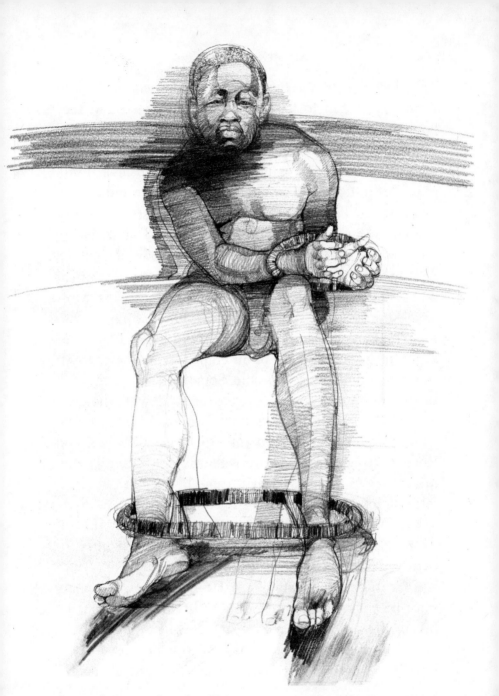

Some of the people captured in wars were sold to the Europeans as slaves. Many African societies were disrupted by the slave trade.

competition between eager nations grew worse. And so Europeans began to make drives farther inland and they began to fight the people they met, and to conquer and colonize the various lands and societies.

By the nineteenth century, with trade flourishing, Europeans began to take more interest in the nature and character of Africa. Travelers wrote back about the strange people and customs they had seen; men like René Caillié, Henry Barth, and Mungo Park spent long periods of time in African cities and towns, and published detailed journals that read like fairy tales to the astonished Europeans. Most of all, missionaries went to Africa. Some had come with the traders; some had come to preach to lonely Europeans at the forts and outposts of an empire. Most were set on converting thousands of people. Some African Kings, such as those of the Bakongo, were impressed with these religious men, seeing them as the possessors of all Western knowledge. They sent their sons to Lisbon, Madrid, and Rome to be educated as early as the sixteenth century, and in some cases these Africans became bishops in the Catholic Church.

Missionary interest in Africa was cultural and, most of all, religious, but it often led the way to the conquest of Africa. David Livingstone, a missionary, stayed in South and Central Africa many years. He failed as a missionary since he converted almost no one to Christianity, but he became famous as an explorer. Suddenly he dropped out of sight. All of Europe began to wonder at his absence and his silence, and finally an American businessman named

Henry Stanley set out after him. Stanley traveled from East to West Africa, and as he moved across the land he signed treaties with African Kings and chiefs, treaties that promised to place them under European protection. While Stanley conducted business on one side of the Congo River, another man named De Brazza was doing similar business on the other side. They were joined by other businessmen, many working on behalf of European governments. They promised the Africans protection of all kinds: protection from civil war; protection from other Europeans; protection from the Arab slavers; and, finally, protection from themselves. When some Africans balked, as in the western Sudan, claiming that they needed no outside help, help was forced upon them. In fighting to conquer the western Sudan, General Faidherbe, a Frenchman, gave up claiming that he was bringing them peace and stated bluntly that he was bringing them "powder."

And so Africa was carved up among many European nations, which secured them steady markets for products. But they found that they were wasting time and energy squabbling with each other, fighting over countries and booty. At last, a conference to settle the matter was called, and in Berlin, Germany, in 1884–85, the countries of Europe officially divided Africa among themselves. This done, they renewed their wars with African rulers in West, South, Central, and East Africa, and defeated and exiled most of them. Samoray Touré of Guinea was sent to Gabon, the Ashantehene of the Ashanti was sent to the Seychelles Islands; King Jaja of Opobo, Nigeria, was sent to the West Indies, and King Behanzin of Dahomey to Martinique, also in the West Indies. Then the Europeans set about securing their economic gains.

Large farms were established in East Africa. Land was seized for farms and pastures in South Africa. Rubber was taken from the Congo forests by forcing villagers, on pain of severe punishment, to collect pounds of it. Diamond, gold, and copper mines were opened in South Africa and Zambia. Africans were assigned land and told to grow certain crops; they were moved from rural areas to mines, plantations, and ports. The Europeans took over African towns such as Jenne, Kano and Timbuktu, then built their own and induced Africans to move there by taxing them in currency that could not be gotten in the country districts. Africans began to pour into Dakar, Abidjan, Accra, Lagos, Johannesburg, Pretoria, Nairobi, all European-built towns, and new centers of government, trade, commerce and alien ways of life.

The African subsistence economies based on trading goods and food, were forced to change into ones that required the exchange of money. And as people left their homes and villages to go to town to make money they were drawn into town life and settled. They sent word back to their friends and relatives, who came too. Many Africans soon realized money could be made by planting new kinds of crops. And so in Ghana, Kwashe Tete founded the cocoa industry, planting the beans among his own Ashanti people. Cocoa became an African enterprise. In Kenya, the Kikuyu tried to make coffee an African enterprise, but the Europeans did not like this competition. They claimed that the Kikuyu couldn't use the proper modern methods to plant coffee, and would thus encourage the spread of disease. In this way they were able to stop the Kikuyu from selling their coffee to other countries throughout the world. The same thing was attempted in Tanzania, though in Uganda the Europeans failed to prevent the Ugandans from growing their own cotton.

Africans had to deal with European traders in order to reach the markets of the West. And many of these Africans, exposed to the chance of earning a living in new ways and for new reasons, accepted the opportunity eagerly. Finally, they did become a part of the world market. Thus cocoa from farms in Ghana is made into Hershey bars in Bethlehem, Pennsylvania, and rubber from Liberia goes to the Firestone Company. African economies became linked to those of the West and suffered when the stock market crashed.

Economic changes—new crops, money, new kinds of work—never take place without social and cultural ones, too. Africans moving into towns were met by missionaries bringing word of a new religion and a new civilization. Missionaries had very different ideas on family, child-rearing, and marriage. They hated polygyny (having more than one wife), which was the normal African marriage pattern, and they did their best to persuade Africans to forsake it for monogamy, and release their extra wives. The missionaries did not understand (or perhaps care) that the bride token was a central part of African social life, involving families and vows of respect and mutual cooperation as well as two marriage partners. Missionaries knew only a patrilineal society, but many African children belonged to their mothers' families, with the mother's brother being as important as their father.

Missionaries insisted that Africans adopt European names, and felt that European methods of education should be instituted. Traditional African education bound work and life together. One was educated as one lived. European education, on the other hand, was highly structured, more so than the bush schools. The subjects taught were quite removed from day-to-day living. African children were taken from their families to attend Western schools. This situation helped to tear apart the traditional family organization. African parents saw no sense in this, for what good family would give away a child to be reared and taught by strangers? They often saw this recruitment as little different from recruitment of their contemporaries for labor migration. School was a kind of labor recruitment in the eyes of many people, and the system of education was entirely unfair, for many of the children sent away to school were expected to work in the mines or offices of the towns, and not to return home to their family.

Africans noticed too that European education was not doing all that it promised in terms of training Africans to get ahead in their rapidly changing world. No matter how well their children did in school, the best jobs were still taken by Europeans. The schools for African children only went up to a certain grade. African children were not being permitted to be educated past a certain point decided upon by the European educators. And yet, Western education was too firmly established to return to traditional African education. So mothers began to collect money rather than goods in the markets to send their children to England, France, and America for the best Western education.

With children leaving home, and husbands and wives often separated because of work, African kinship systems were weakened greatly. Africans had had large families, descended from a common, revered ancestor. They had always lived in compounds and villages, or in closely knit town wards. With the rise of the new towns, the importance of the individual (seen most, traditionally, in the marketplaces), increased too. Africans began to live more by themselves and work for themselves; the extended family began to shrivel and lose much of its meaning. "Mother" began to mean one's biological mother only, not mother's sisters as well. European languages were spoken more and more, and so European kinship terms were used and accepted.

African political institutions were ignored, manipulated, or destroyed as the Europeans took over. Kings had no importance once they had been conquered by the Europeans; they were seen as chiefs, though they often kept their old titles in the eyes of their own people. Europeans played down the importance of African nobility, and often created chiefs of their own in order to help the Europeans rule with more success and security. Among the Igbo of Nigeria, these "manufactured" chiefs were legion, and they were carefully used in a system of Indirect rule. When the provincial administrator received orders from the British governor, he passed them on to his district officer, as well as to the local King. The district officer took the message to a local chief he worked with, while the King sent the message through his own bureaucracy of ministers and chiefs, down to the district chief. And so, traditional political systems existed, but at the same time, did not exist. They were both strengthened and weakened. On the one hand, African subjects could no longer rid themselves of an unworthy or exploitative ruler. On the other hand, Europeans could get rid of him immediately if the need arose, and so his power among his subjects was consistently weakened. People with different rulers, from different places, found themselves crowded together in the same towns and areas as strangers. Their main link was the fact that they were subjects of the French, the Portuguese, the British, or the Belgians.

Those educated Africans who left to go to America, Britain, and France for higher education met New World Africans, the descendants of those who had left Africa centuries ago. Some of them had heard of those New World Africans who had been missionaries in West, Central, and South Africa. Others had heard of men like Paul Cuffee, a Massachusetts ship captain who took fellow blacks to Sierra Leone and Liberia and encouraged others to follow them; and like Martin Delany, a doctor, who had planned to settle among the Egba people in Nigeria. But many Africans were meeting New World blacks for the first time face to face.

These two groups of Africans were similar and yet different. The New World Africans had been Westernized too, since they lived in the West, but they saw Westerners differently and from a closer angle. They looked back to

Africa in a way that native Africans didn't. They saw the continent as a whole, not as a collection of parts ruled over by different countries thousands of miles away. Continental Africans mostly saw just their own countries or certain groups of colonies. Some Africans knew only about the French colonies, others only about the English. A French West African was likely to know more about France than about the neighboring British-ruled Gold Coast; for many Africans had arrived overseas with a European-African education that had taught them they were, or should try to be, part of Europe's heritage. French Africans spoke of their Gallic ancestors with blond hair and blue eyes. Often they believed that they were nearly European. But the Europeans they met did not believe this at all, nor did the Afro-Americans and Afro-West Indians they met. And so, continental Africans and those Africans in the diaspora (outside) rediscovered each other, and began to feel a kind of African unity that included at least three continents. They called it Pan-Africanism. Africans from the continent began to see their land as a non-European whole. They wanted to rediscover and re-create their civilizations; they were willing to be nationalistic; they wanted independence.

Those Africans who returned home in the 1930s, with their law degrees and their teaching certificates from top foreign universities, began to challenge the legality of the European administrators and African rulers (whom they saw as stooges). They fought for new constitutions and for more African participation in legislative councils. Yet, they too were partly Westernized, and so their attacks were sometimes confused or muted. It was not until after World

War II that these intellectuals began to find the support they needed to bring about real changes. To their surprise, their supporters were not the educated, newly created middle class or bourgeoisie, nor the disgruntled, deposed Kings and chiefs. Their strongest supporters were the Africans, often uneducated, who had begun to move from the rural lands and villages to the commercial towns and cities. These people were more militant, more nationalistic, than the middle class and the chiefs; in some ways they were more unhappy with their lives.

For the first time then, Europeans found their authority seriously challenged; they found themselves fighting the transfer of their ruling rights to Africans. And the chiefs, their ambiguous allies, found themselves fighting to prevent the shift of their limited power to developing African political parties. These parties claimed that they, not the Europeans, nor the traditional rulers who worked with them, represented the needs and wishes of the people. They promised to govern fairly and to modernize Africa without betraying her past. Africans started to fight Africans for political power, and as some political leaders won, they tried to see that no other Africans, especially those who had opposed them at any time, came to power. But by doing this, they often found almost no restraints on them —a very different situation from that of traditional Africa, where the King, no matter how powerful, always had certain checks and balances on his actions.

It was and it is a very complicated situation. Political independence from the countries of Europe did not erase the problems colonization had created. African peoples are still struggling with the problems of both. They are very anxious that those Africans in South Africa (Azania), South-West Africa (Namibia), and Rhodesia (Zimbabwe), as well as Angola, Mozambique, and Guinea-Bissau should be free. They despise *apartheid*, a system practiced in South Africa and Rhodesia that keeps Africans from having equal rights in their own countries. They are concerned about what kinds of governments they will have, and about whether the armies that have seized power in many countries will give it back to civilian people. They worry about the ethnic divisions in their societies which, in the past, have led to civil war in Zaire and Nigeria, and they worry about the inter-ethnic strife between Hutu and Tutsi people in Ruanda and Burundi. They are disturbed by the divisions among African societies and states—divisions that existed long before the Europeans arrived, though in different forms. Can these be ignored or erased? Can small states compete and survive in the modern world? Can different languages, customs, and notions of civilization exist without bringing about conflicts? Can economics bound to Europe separate themselves successfully?

These are important questions and outward-looking questions. But following independence, Africans also had to look inward at their culture to see what had happened to it. What of their former religions? Europeans had not appreciated or approved of African religion at all. Europeans saw God in a different way, looking over their shoulders, watching their every action jealously. They con-

demned African divinities and spirits as heathen idols;
they did not realize how seldom they approached their
own God directly. But saints have much in common with
African divinities; Mary is not unlike Ale, the earth goddess; Europeans, like Africans, have statues and carry med-
als or charms.

Africans resented this disrespect for their religions, and
they did not always like the tenets of Catholic and Protes-
tant beliefs. They saw nothing in the Bible that forbade
polygyny—did not Solomon and David have many wives?
The Bible taught that all people were equal before God,
and Africans learned this in missionary Sunday schools.
Yet Europeans discriminated against them; the Church
itself did not want to accept African priests. The Bible
spoke of the "meek inheriting the earth," and told of Ethiopia stretching forth her hand to God. Africans saw themselves as the meek ones and the chosen ones. They could
not reconcile this with the actions of the European Church,
and so many of them left to form churches of their own.
Some of them came to America, and their deacons con-
tacted the African Methodist Episcopal churches in the
United States and exchanged ideas with them. Other
Africans solved the conflict simply by continuing to worship their own deities, regardless of missionary and Church
opposition. Shango, Ale, and Mawu-Lisa are still wor-
shiped; the rainbow is still seen as a magical sign. Islam
continues to thrive, though it has had to deal with modern education and ideas. More and more Africans, despite
their exposure to Christianity, are looking to their tradi-

tional religions with new respect, discovering their beauty and diversity all over again.

Art, so linked with religion, has changed too, but it is finding new strength in its traditions. Europeans had not only wanted Africans to change their gods, they had also wanted them to change their strongest images of themselves and their universe. They gave Africans saints' names and demanded that they abandon the worship of their ancestors. Statues lost their sacred meaning and became mere objects; temples, altars, masks, and sculptured figures did too. Art was separated from everyday life and so lost its place in religion. Only in the rural areas, which were less affected by the Europeans, did it remain substantially as it had been. Africans who lived in towns and cities abandoned their ceremonies and began to look upon the masks, proverbs, songs, dances, and drums as "primitive," "barbarous," and "heathen."

Oddly enough, it was in traveling to Europe that Africans changed this disdain for their own art. Europeans in Europe resented imitations of themselves; many of them were bored with their own art forms and eager to hear about new ones. European artists and scholars discovered new models and ideas in African art, new meanings and conceptions of form and space, new visions of art's place in day-to-day living. They tried to quiz Africans about these things and many Africans were embarrassed to know so little about their own culture, or to have deliberately forgotten it. Thus on return to Africa they had to go to the rural areas, where people still practiced traditional re-

The old and the new exist side by side in Africa's large cities. The continent is a land of contrasts.

ligion and still sang, danced, and made music in the old ways. Contemporary Africans, seeking to see their land as a unique whole, look to art as an expression of African philosophy, character, and aesthetics.

The old is blending with the new in African art and architecture, perhaps more harmoniously than in any other part of African life. Ancient art motifs are seen on airplanes and buildings; modern dances, which came from an African base and are learned in America, are joined once more to their ancestral stream. African-American music, the real American folk art, has found its way to Africa and given new life to its ancestor. Traditional plays are modernized, and they treat contemporary African themes: marriage, civil war, and the conflicts of changing cultures. African ballet companies are taking their art into the Western world and bringing that of the West back home again. Meanwhile, the New World Africans are growing ever more conscious of their ancestral roots in time. They too are now appreciating as their own the ancient traditions of Africa. They now see beauty in their faces, their hair, and in the unique synthesis they have made of contrasting Old and New World cultures. Many African-Americans believe that a meaningful future for them can only be one that reflects this synthesis, and their belief is shared by Africans. A group of African villagers today may listen eagerly to the sounds of a jazz band, then move outside to drum and dance.

It is possible for the old and the new to exist in peace; it is possible to blend the present and the past when creating a future; and it is certainly possible to draw inspiration from the "roots of time." Such contradictions and syntheses have always been a part of Africa's history, but they are being faced now in a new and intense way. Africans, like African-Americans, are seeking to blend the best of the traditional with the best of the modern. It is not an easy task. But Africans have a proverb that says, "Things gained easily disappear easily."

GUIDE TO PRONUNCIATION

Ale	ah-lay
amala oha	ah-mah-la o-ha
Amene	ah-may-nay
Batwa	bah-twa
chi	chee
dipo	dee-po
Dopkwe	dop-k-way
Egbe	egg-bay
Ekine	eh-kee-nay
griot	gree-ot
Hausa	how-za
Ibini Okpade	ee-bee-nee ok-pah-day
ikula	ee-ku-la
Jie	ji
Jukun	ju-kuhn
Lovedu	lo-vay-du
Luvale	lu-vah-lay
malweza	mahl-way-za
Masai	mah-sí
Mende	men-day
Mossi	móø-see

ndanga	n-dan-ga
ndichie	n-dee-chee
Ngai	n-guy
nkomi	n-ko-mee
Nupe	nu-pay
okparas	ok-pah-ras
Onyankopon	on-yah-ko-pong
walo	wah-lo
warri	war-ri
Yoruba	yúr-u-ba
Zaire	za-eere

INDEX

Central Africa, 13, 22, 90, 106, 107
(*see also* individual people, places);
markets, 41
"Ceremony of the Lions," 24
Chiefs, 56, 62, 68–69, 114; Europeans
and, 107, 111–12, 114
Childhood, birth and, 16–26 (*see also*
Children, African); and adulthood,
22–26; childbirth, 17–20; growing
up, 20–26; initiation ceremonies,
22–26; naming of, 17–18; puberty
rituals, 21–25; toilet training, 20;
weaning, 20
Children, African: and age sets,
25–26; birth and childhood, 16–26
(*see also* Childhood); European
influence on family life and, 109–
11; and kinship and marriage, 45ff.;
and politics and society, 56–57;
and storytelling, 84–85
Chorophones (stringed instruments),
91–92
Christianity, 80–82, 101, 106, 109,
115–17
Circumcision, 21–22, 24
Click languages, 12–13
Cloth weaving, 39, 96
Cocoa, 108, 109
Coffee growing, 108–9
Congo-Kordofanian languages, 12
Coptic Christianity, 80
Courts, 60–62, 68–69, 77, 94
Crafts, 38–41; guilds, 40
Crimes (wrongdoing), punishment
and, 57–62, 68–69; religious
beliefs and, 73–77
Crops, 10–11, 27, 37–38 (*see also*
specific kinds); Europeans and
changes in, 108, 109

Dahomey, 36–37, 70, 71, 73, 77,
91, 96, 108
Dances (dancing), 83–84, 86, 87,
88, 90, 94, 96, 117, 119; Kalabari
masques, 97–99
Dark Child, The (Laye), 24
Death, African beliefs and customs
and, 74, 78–80; burials and
funerals, 78–80
Decisions (decision-making), 56–
69. *See also* Rulers (ruling)
Didinga, the, 90
Dinka, the, 34, 72
Dogon, the, 22, 71, 73
Drums (drumming), 92–94, 97, 117,

119; and communicating, 92–94;
kinds, 92

Earth (*see also* Farming; Land):
beliefs concerning, 36, 70–73
East Africa, 34, 37, 100, 107, 108;
markets, 41
Ebrie, the, 10
Economy (economic systems),
African, 27–44; Europeans and,
108–9
Education, 110–11, 112, 113–14
Egbe, the, 38
Egypt, 9, 12, 13, 64–65, 80
Ekine masques, 97–99
Ekoi, the, 83
Elders, 56–62, 66, 67, 68
Ethiopia, 80–81, 116
Europe (European influences), 15,
101–15 (*see also* specific aspects,
countries); political independence
from, 113–15; religion and, 80–
82, 115–17
Extended family, 37, 49 (*see also*
Family); European influence on,
111

Face and body decorating, 95–96
Family (family life), African:
childhood and, 16–17; death and
burial and, 78–80; European
influence on, 109–11; kinship and
marriage and, 45–55; politics and
society and, 56–69
Fanti, the, 45, 56, 103
Farming, 10–11, 12, 28, 35–39
Father's sister, role of, 48
Fishing, 10, 11, 12
Fon, the, 70, 71, 73, 77
Food (food gathering), 10, 11, 27,
32–38 (*see also* specific kinds);
bartering and, 35–36
Forests, 27–28, 29
France, 101, 112, 113
Fulani, the, 10, 11, 13, 34
Funerals, burials and, 78–80

Galla, the, 26
Gama, Vasco da, 101, 102
Ghana, 9, 16, 45, 56, 64, 72, 87,
91, 108, 109; Empire, end of, 103
Gift-giving, 50–53, 54
God(s), 13, 16, 17, 18, 27–28, 63,
64; in African art, 83–84, 86, 94,
95; in African religion, 70–78, 80,
81–82, 115–17